MULTICAMPUS LIBRARIES:
Organization and Administration Case Studies

by
RUTH SCHWARTZ

The Scarecrow Press, Inc.
Metuchen, N.J., & London
1988

Library of Congress Cataloging-in-Publication
   Data

Schwartz, Ruth.
   Multicampus libraries : organization and
   administration case studies / by Ruth
   Schwartz.
        p.   cm.
   Bibliography: p.
   Includes index.
   ISBN 0-8108-2173-7
   1. Libraries, University and college--
Administration--Case studies. I. Title.
Z675.U5S336 1988
027.7--dc19   88-21910

Copyright © 1988 by Ruth Schwartz
Manufactured in the United States of America

TABLE OF CONTENTS

	Page
FIGURES	v
ACKNOWLEDGEMENTS	vii

Chapter

- I. INTRODUCTION ... 1
- II. INSTITUTION I (HARRISON UNIVERSITY) ... 29
  - The Environment: The University and Its Setting ... 29
  - The University Libraries: Structures and Processes ... 44
- III. INSTITUTION II (CLEMENS UNIVERSITY) ... 92
  - The Environment: the University and Its Setting ... 92
  - The University Libraries: Structures and Processes ... 112
- IV. INSTITUTION III (CHASE UNIVERSITY) ... 159
  - The Environment: the University and Its Setting ... 159
  - The University Libraries: Structures and Processes ... 177
- V. SUMMARY AND CONCLUSIONS ... 217

BIBLIOGRAPHY ... 244

APPENDIX
  Sample interview questionnaire ... 249

INDEX ... 256

FIGURES

Figure		Page
1.	Harrison University: Distances Between Campuses by Auto Route	30
2.	Organization Chart: Harrison University, Office of the President	37
3.	Organization Chart: Harrison University Libraries	55
4.	Organization Chart: Harrison University, Office of the Provost	57
5.	Clemens University: Distances between Campuses by Auto Route	93
6.	Organization Chart: Clemens University	99
7.	Organization Chart: Clemens University, Thoreau Campus Library	115
8.	Organization Chart: Clemens University, Emerson Campus Library	117
9.	Organization Chart: Clemens University, Cooper Campus Library	119
10.	Chase University: Distances between Campuses by Auto Route	160
11.	Organization Chart: Chase University	170

12. Organization Chart: Chase University, Bethlehem Campus Library ___184

13. Organization Chart: Chase University, Kodak Campus Library ___185

14. Organization chart: Chase University, Dupont Campus Library ___186

ACKNOWLEDGEMENTS

I am profoundly grateful to the many people who have played an important role, individually and collectively, in the development of this dissertation. Some must remain anonymous, a few I am privileged to identify.

"Thank you" to the seventy-eight academic administrators and librarians who generously shared their time and their enthusiasms with me.

"Thank you" to the defense committee for their important contribution to the dissertation process.

"Thank you" to Professor R. Kathleen Molz for serving as second reader and offering both objective criticism and sympathetic encouragement.

And a heart-felt "thank you" to Professor Phyllis Dain, under whose direction the dissertation was written. Her acute observations, her advice and guidance laced with patience and humor sustained me throughout this project.

"Thank you" to my son, Peter, whose knowledge of the arcane workings of my word processor he shared with me, enabling me to endlessly mold and shape my expressed thoughts into coherent meaning. To my other children, Natasha, Bob and Nina "thank you" for your gentle encouragement and quiet pride. And to little Jenna Lee my deepest "thank you". Your smiles and chortles brighten my days.

Above all, to my husband I wish to say: "Thank you. You may now put the apron aside. I am going back to cooking again."

CHAPTER I

INTRODUCTION

Background

The beginning of the true "university" system in the history of American higher education is not clear cut. Many universities of today were founded in the colonial period as colleges in which the academic focus was to educate a group of learned men for the ministry and for leadership in society generally. The term "university," although used earlier, did not acquire its modern connotation--an institution offering advanced professional and graduate degrees, in particular the Ph.D.[1]--until the last quarter of the nineteenth century. In that period new universities such as Cornell and Johns Hopkins were founded, and old colleges began to be transformed into universities. In the development of universities this movement to combine schools and graduate programs can be considered the forerunner of multicampus institutions.

After World War II the unparalleled growth of American higher education produced a pattern of organization that is today's multicampus university system, described by Eugene C. Lee and Frank M. Bowen, the authors of the first major study of such systems, as "the grouping of individual campuses under a common framework of governance."[2] Lee and Bowen found multicampus universities developed in two distinct patterns: "Consolidated systems resulted from the aggregation under a new central administration and governing board, of previously existing campuses. Flagship systems resulted from the extension of an established campus into a system either by the creation of new campuses or the absorption of old ones."[3] Edward G. Holley identified this organizational entity as consisting of either new branches of major universities, an expansion of former small colleges, or conversion of several private universities into public institutions.[4] By the 1970s multicampus universities had an enrollment of 40% of all students; more than one-fifth of all campuses were integral parts of such systems.[5] While many multicampus universities have non-urban campuses, often as the flagship or the primary, dominant campus, the multicampus is to a great extent an urban development.[6] The increased enrollment of the 1960s compelled many urban universities to expand,[7] and William B. Birenbaum reports that in the 1960s universities were actually seeking urban campuses.[8] In the early 1970s many urban-based universities further expanded into suburbia as population shifts occurred.

The multicampus system is related to another product of the expansionary 1960s, the "multiversity," which is defined as the "complex, multipurpose campus."[9] The difference between the multiversity and the multicampus university is geographical. A multiversity consists of graduate programs, undergraduate colleges, professional schools, and other units in one geographical location and exhibits a "more or less peaceful coexistence of a number of academically distinct communities."[10] The multicampus university implies "similar coexistence of geographically distinct communities."[11] While not all multiversities therefore are multicampus universities, almost all multicampus universities can be considered multiversities, since they

Introduction

often are comprised of large, complex single campuses plus various other campuses.

Private and public multicampus universities came into existence during a period of financial well-being for academic institutions that was due in part to increased federal funding, sharp growth in the student population, and acceptance of the idea of near universal access to higher education.[12] Not only were there more students in academia than ever before in history, but they also included students of "many more levels of academic ability and academic preparation than in earlier times, from many more cultural backgrounds, and with more diverse career goals."[13] For such a student body the multicampus comprehensive university by its very nature and special structure offers diversity of campuses, specialization of campuses, and opportunity for cooperation among campuses.[14] Although most of the multicampus universities are public institutions, private institutions as well have adopted this form, but in fewer numbers. Lee and Bowen identified in 1971 fifty-four public and nine private multicampus universities.[15]

The growth of academic libraries has paralleled the growth of higher education. The American college library can be said to have been born in 1638 when John Harvard bequeathed one-half of his estate and all of his books to the college that had been founded two years earlier. College libraries grew slowly during the first half of the nineteenth century with collections that consisted mostly of standard titles, theology, law and medical books. Toward the end of the nineteenth century academic collections grew in size, scope, and complexity of organization as colleges became universities and college libraries transformed themselves into university libraries.

In this century, libraries experienced a phenomenal growth as higher education expanded. After World War II the unprecedented increase in college and university enrollment and the expansion of graduate education demanded determined measures by librarians to enlarge entire collections,[16] construct new buildings, and increase their staffs and services. Grants of federal funds in the 1960s helped;[17] the multicampus university libraries were major recipients of such grants.

Libraries that were geographically separated on multiple campuses of a university governed by a single administration became the multicampus library systems of the recent decades. They and single campus university libraries have shared a common goal: to serve the educational and research needs of students, faculty and researchers in the university. Similarly, the libraries have faced common problems: space demands created by the large number of volumes that were added, escalating costs of titles and materials, the management of larger staffs and increased user needs, and adaptation of computer technology to library operations. As of the 1970s, most universities and their libraries have been confronted with the need to engage in strategic planning to accommodate declining enrollments and fiscal stringency.

Beyond the commonality of problems faced by the multicampus university library and the single campus university library are issues inherent in the multicampus library system: the degree of centralization versus local autonomy, the nature of power and control as influenced by the parent organization, and the patterns of internal organization of multicampus libraries that reflect the issue of whether centralization or decentralization is better suited to meet an institution's educational objectives.[18] The location of one campus in relation to another has affected

Introduction

the administrative control of library systems and the delegation and extent of authority. According to J. Michael Bruno, "Administrative control over all units on campus is much easier to achieve than the extension of such control over libraries which may be located ten or twenty miles away."[19]

Centralization can mean strong administrative centralization--control of a number of campus libraries by a central library administration with local campus libraries maintaining a minimum level of autonomy[20]--or operational centralization with certain operations performed in a single place for the various units of a system.[21] In a decentralized library system local autonomy is maintained at the campus level while the central administration serves as a coordinating agency. Another alternative in a multicampus university system is the existence of local autonomy without any central administration. The centralization/decentralization theme appears throughout this study, as it constituted a focal point in discussions of governance and control in various campus libraries among the multicampus systems studied. In recent years technological advances have worked in favor of decentralization.[22] For example, with the advent of the automated online catalog, and with rapid document delivery, a former argument against decentralization may no longer apply as the ability exists, in a way not possible before, to locate and request an item from any campus location through a computer based catalog of all campus library holdings.

There have been, also, experiments in the degree of administrative control of libraries within a multicampus university system. Historically the problems of organization and administration have increased as institutions have grown in complexity and physical resources. This study should help determine under what conditions and to what degree libraries in a multicampus system derive more or less autonomy as a result of campus and system-wide policies and directions. Since multicampus libraries are likely to be reflections of multicampus university organization, they can be included in the following statement:

> The central question about any multicampus system is whether it improves results--particularly the adequacy of advance planning, the enhancement of diversity and quality, the effective use of resources, and the successful representation to external authorities--more than it impedes the processes of governance.[23]

Previous Studies

Since libraries tend to reflect the administration and organization of their parent institutions, it is necessary to be aware of the problems of multicampus university administration before undertaking a study of multicampus libraries. Literature concerning the nature and scope of the multicampus university is limited, with only two major studies available. The first significant examination of the multicampus revolution in university organization was Lee and Bowen's The Multicampus University: A Study of Academic Governance, sponsored by the Carnegie Commission on Higher Education in 1971.[24] Lee and Bowen evaluated the advantages and disadvantages of the American multicampus system as they examined in detail the history and organization, governance and administration of nine multicampus state universities: the Universities of California, Illinois, Missouri, North Carolina, Texas, Wisconsin, the State and City Universities of New York, and the California State University and College System. Over a period of two years the authors conducted a series of extensive personal interviews with campus and institutional personnel "... not to produce a detailed and accurate survey of each phase of administration in each university but, rather, to see the overall picture, the broad dimensions of multicampus organization."[25]

Their study undertook to examine each of these public universities in three areas:

(1) Environment: the environment of the multicampus university governance, both external and internal, with emphasis upon the impact of state government and statewide organization of higher education;

(2) Structures: the multicampus university governing structures--governing boards, central administration, systemwide faculty and study organizations;

(3) Processes: the processes of academic governance in multicampus university systems, including academic plans, budget administration, admissions, faculty and administrative personnel, public and governmental relations, and business affairs.

Lee and Bowen summarized the strengths and weaknesses of the large state-supported multicampus university. As strengths they identified new campus acquisitions and development; campus specialization, diversity, and cooperation in academic planning and budget preparation; quality control of new graduate degree programs; efficiencies in university business management; and enhanced public and governmental relations. The major weaknesses of multicampus universities were absence of agreement on the relative authority of the state government, the coordinating agency, and the university over the governance of the university system; the state government's inadequate delegation of fiscal authority to the university; inadequate indices of budgeting support; lack of innovation in academic planning and programs; governing boards that do not function as multicampus system boards; and political pressures from state government.[26]

In 1975 Lee and Bowen published the results of their follow-up examination of the nine multicampus public university systems first examined by them in 1971.[27] Their report deals with planning for a period characterized by limited growth, fiscal constraints, unstable enrollments, and possible retrenchment. Through questionnaires and personal interviews, Lee and Bowen found major changes: increased emphasis on academic planning and academic program review, on academic budgeting, on program development, and regional coordination. The researchers produced a model for an exemplary multicampus system, aware of the fact that the balance between centralization and campus authority must vary among systems.

Lee and Bowen have been so far the only researchers to provide extensive insight into the administration of multicampus universities. The only other book on the subject is a short commentary, Multiple Campuses, published in 1964, by Peter Sammartino, then president of Fairleigh Dickinson University, who briefly discussed the origins of multicampus institutions and their governance.[28]

Other writers have added some background to an overall study of multicampus institutions; several books on higher education include chapters on multicampus systems. Algo D. Henderson and Jean G. Henderson, "Interinstitutional Coordination, Multicampus Systems" in Higher Education in America, described the growth of publicly supported multicampus systems since World War II and discussed the advantages and disadvantages of a

Introduction

central administration with a single board. They concluded that such a governance structure is desirable even though there is the danger that it can become too powerful and too large.[29] Leonard E. Goodall, "Intercampus Relations In Multicampus Universities" in <u>Crisis In Campus Management</u>, presents observations based upon his own experience as a member of the faculty and administration of Michigan-Dearborn and the University of Illinois at Chicago.[30] He lists the following causative factors in the development of the new urban campuses: the growing population and increased enrollments, the specific need of an urban population for preparation for employment, the resistance to high tuition at private institutions, and the desire for a degree from a major public university in a state. Among the problems that occurred when some major universities became multicampus insitutitions, Goodall notes, are the concern by the senior campus that the new campus will diminish its reputation and reduce its resources, the belief of the new campus that it can become an "instant university," and the need for a precise definition of the campus mission.[31] This researcher noted the same concern by the senior campuses in the three multicampus institutions of this study.

Several doctoral dissertations have addressed aspects of multicampus institutions. Robert C. Keys examined the administrative structures of ninety two-year and four-year public multicampus colleges and universities with the objective of developing a model of the decision-making authority given to the campuses by the institutional system.[32] The institutional activities were grouped into five functional areas: academic affairs, student affairs, business and financial affairs, administrative and auxiliary affairs, and external affairs. The results indicated that campuses in four-year institutions had more decision-making authority than did campuses in two-year colleges, although the degree of campus authority varied--greatest for student affairs and least in the area of business and financial affairs. Sean Van Pallandt analyzed the current status of systemwide self-studies of selected multicampus universities, determining the objectives, the methods, and the usefulness of the systemwide self-study approach to the multicampus university administration.[33] William Wade Waymer examined the extent of actual involvement of central administrations in the accrediting process and the degree to which they should be involved.[34] Patrick Roy Lake studied six multicampus community colleges in three states to identify what problems were experienced and how they were resolved when a single campus community college became a multicampus institution.[35]

An article written in 1985 by John W. Creswell, Ronald W. Roskens, and Thomas C. Henry[36] states that in spite of the growth in the number of public and private multicampus institutions we know very little in the 1980s about the different forms of multicampus institutions. The authors are particularly concerned that no scheme or "typology" has been developed to identify structures of the institutions for purposes of comparison with peer or comparable multicampus institutions. For this reason, the authors developed a typology and definition of multicampus systems based upon four organizational and administrative characteristics: (1) control of the system--public or private; (2) jurisdiction of the board--statewide or less than statewide in scope; (3) comparability of campuses within the system--homogeneous or heterogeneous; and (4) administrative structure of the system--flagship or a separate central office. Using this typology, they produced a list of multicampus systems in existence at the time of their writing that differentiated between private systems, statewide systems,

Introduction   11

heterogeneous public systems and homogeneous
public systems. However, they acknowledged
that changes are occurring constantly and expect that the typology they have developed
will be a reference point for future research
on multicampus systems. The article "affirms
the importance of studying systems as a unit
of analysis and as a way of exploring characteristics that differentiate among the
types."[37]

The professional literature on libraries
in a multicampus university is not extensive.
(None of the existing studies of multicampus
universities encompassed their libraries; Lee
and Bowen explicitly omitted libraries from
their scope.) The only full-scale study of
the libraries of a multicampus university library sytem is <u>Coordination: Concept or Reality? A Study of Libraries in a University System</u> by William J. Myrick, Jr.[38] This work
focused on the history of efforts to effect
cooperation and coordination among the autonomous libraries of the colleges that comprised the new City University of New York
formed in 1961. In chronicling and analyzing
the crucial first ten years of the Council of
Chief Librarians of the City University,
Myrick found the outcome to be negative in
terms of achieving coordination, and for the
following reasons: 1) institutional autonomy,
2) librarians' negative attitudes, 3) lack of
library support by the central university administration, and 4) lack of a full-time central coordinating agency with sufficient authority.

Donald L. Ryan surveyed by questionnaire
twenty-four libraries of "off-campus units,"
almost all of which had been developed after
World War II. He defined such units as "institutions which are under the sponsorship
of, and bear the name of, a larger college or
university located elsewhere and which offer
at least a two-year undergraduate liberal

arts curriculum to full-time day students."[39] The results of the questionnaire, answered by eighteen libraries, identified problems and decisions faced by multicampus libraries: growth of collections, extent of duplication of collections, determination of areas of specialization, centralization or decentralization of services, administrative lines and policies.

One unpublished report germane to this research is the "Report of the Provost's Task Force on University Libraries" (Pennsylvania State University), September 18, 1981.[40] The task force had been appointed to offer recommendations to ameliorate the problems in governing the multicampus libraries of Pennsylvania State University. After surveying acquisition priorities, the most effective use of library budgets, and the mechanics of administering scattered campus libraries, the task force urged the establishment of a new position of director of all university libraries. In their opinion this centralization of authority would eliminate the problems arising from uncoordinated and duplicative administrations. In 1983 James Neal and Barbara Smith published a study of the collection support available for faculty research at the branch campuses of Pennsylvania State University.[41] Using citation analysis of journal articles published by the faculty and a questionnaire, they determined that a high percentage of the material used in their research by faculty working at the branch libraries was indeed available through intercampus and interlibrary loans. Recommendations were made to encourage faculty to participate in the development of the central research collections for greater fulfillment of intercampus loans and to expand reciprocal borrowing agreements of resources with other major university libraries in the state.

Introduction

Although somewhat dated, John F. McDonald's "The Rutgers University Library: A Study of Current Problems of Organization and Service in a Decentralized University" is relevant.[42] His analysis offers suggestions for similar studies of multicampus libraries without making specific recommendations for operational improvement. Of more current value is the "Rutgers University Libraries Master Plan," developed in 1979 by a committee of library directors and others, which deals with the interrelationship of libraries in a multicampus university. In a consideration of the issues--library collections, personnel, automation, facilities, public and technical services, structure and organization--the drafters of the plan provide both historical perspective and current insight into the state of operational affairs of a major multicampus university library system.[43]

Statement of the Problem

Multicampus university systems are a contemporary reality in higher education; they appear to be here to stay despite the current declining enrollments, program reductions, and financial exigencies. While their future cannot be predicted, some conclusions based upon the Lee and Bowen studies can be drawn tentatively about them: multicampus universities have placed increasing emphasis upon academic plans and planning procedures, and their system of governance seems to be working.

Libraries, considered integral to fulfilling the university's mission, were created and collections and services developed to serve the multicampus university institution. Major questions concerning the structure, governance, and future character of the multicampus university library--questions that have been scarcely addressed by students either of higher education or of academic libraries--include:

   --To what extent do the multicampus university libraries mirror their parent institution's governance and structure? Is there an element of political tension among the campuses, and is this reflected within the library system?

   --How have they dealt with expansion? With contraction?

   --Are they a system? Are they interrelated and do they work together as a system, or, if not, are they separate campus libraries held together by some kind of superstructure? To what extent have the libraries been involved in planning on a coordinated and cooperative systemwide basis?

   --How have the libraries dealt with diversification, specialization, resources, and the balance of power?

   --What are the budgeting policies? Does the system have the flexibility to shift appropriated funds among campus libraries to meet changing student demand?

   --What has been the role of new technology and network environment on the libraries on a systemwide basis?

   --What are the levels of autonomy, independence and interdependence? Where is the balance between centralization and local campus authority? What are the lines of authority and reporting?

   --What seem to be the future directions of these libraries, given the contraction in higher education, enrollment trends, and technological developments?

Introduction   15

　　　　　--What other considerations have
surfaced, often unexpectedly, that are unique
to a library system which consists of campuses geographically separated yet administered by one parent body?

　　　　　--To what extent has the history of
the institution and of the libraries themselves played a role in the library's situation?

Aim and Scope

　　　To address the above questions, this research has investigated the broad issues of
administration and governance in multicampus
libraries of three selected multicampus universities, two private and one semi-public,
in the Northeastern United States, using the
case study mode. These libraries represent
two different methods of administration: de-
centralized--campus libraries that have local
campus-based administrative authority, and
centralized--campus libraries that function
within a centrally controlled library system.
One of the private universities (Clemens University)[44] did not have a university librarian at the time of the study; each campus library in its system had an autonomous director. The other private university (Chase
University) has, in contrast, a university
librarian with responsibility and authority
over all the campus libraries. The semi-
public university system selected (Harrison
University) is administered centrally by a
university librarian who is also director of
the main campus library. Common to all the
universities is the addition of two or more
campus libraries to keep pace with the growth
of campuses that occurred after World War II.

　　　The institutions were studied using the
exploratory case method, examining how the
organization and governance of multicampus
libraries related to the structure, govern-

ance, and geography of the parent university, and whether there were significant differences in the administration and organization of the private and semi-public multicampus university library systems. The emphasis has been upon structures and policies, not statistics, upon the determination of goals and the establishment of managerial direction. (Organization charts, for instance, show the chain of command.) At the same time, the pragmatic aspects of duplication of buildings, materials and equipment and the organizational and operational problems of physical decentralization were examined.

The approach developed by Lee and Bowen in their study of multicampus universities has been followed as a model. The investigation and analysis were organized around three basic vantage points:

(1) Environment: revealing and analyzing the environment--the organization and administration of the university in which each library system functions;

(2) Structures: the organization and administrative structure and governance of the libraries, with the lines of responsibility and power;

(3) Processes: collection development, personnel policies, library budget process, cooperation and coordination, technical services and automation.

Methodology

Since to this researcher's knowledge, there have been no comparative studies or general surveys of the governance, administration, and structure of multicampus university libraries, this study has best lent itself to the exploratory case study mode. Although some statistical data were gathered in

Introduction

developing a profile of each institution and its libraries, the basic approach has been qualitative.

Two basic interview formats were used, the selection depending upon the information to be elicited:

--the open-ended confidential interview, flexible and allowing maximum latitude in the areas covered and in the depth of responses;

--a schedule of questions for standard eliciting of facts and descriptions. (For a sample of the interview questionnaire, see Appendix.) Regarding the advantages of the open-ended interview, Harry Levinson states: "... the data are likely to be rich in details .... Only a personal, private interview ... can provide such detailed and refined data.[45] Levinson also suggests that the time for each interview should consist of an hour-and-a-half to two hours with people at the senior executive level, and at least an hour with those below that level.[46]

A three-part research strategy was utilized:

First, to supplement the interviews and provide background information created at the libraries and the institutions, documents (published and unpublished) were examined when available during the visits to each library. Each library had an archival collection, albeit two in greater depth than the third. Major types of documents that were examined include:

--university catalogs
--university archival materials
--university annual reports and
  annual reports of the individual
  libraries

--publications of the libraries
--collection development statements
--accreditation and consultants' reports of the university and its libraries
--other relevant materials

Second, on the basis of the background information, a profile of each university was developed, with sub-profiles of each multicampus library. Data include:

For the university:

--degrees and programs offered
--size of each campus and geographical setting
--number of students and faculty on each campus
--a table of organization, university-wide, including the chief executive officer of the campus

For each library system:

--library services offered
--number and type of library staff
--size and type of collections
--an organizational chart

Third, interviews were held when possible with the following key personnel at each university and library system studied:

--systemwide library directors
--university administrator to whom the director of the university library system reports
--members of the governing bodies of the university
--campus library directors
--campus administrators to whom the campus library directors report
--library staff at the departmental head or divisional head level

Introduction

--other administrative personnel on each campus with familiarity with library policy, organization, etc.

The director of the university libraries of each of the three universities was contacted by telephone requesting permission to use his institution for study; all consented verbally. A week later, a date was made for the first visit and the interview with the chief librarian. In the course of this initial fact-finding meeting a program and schedule were created for subsequent interviews with the personnel selected for the interview process. From January 1985 through January 1986 the investigator visited each of the multicampus university library systems, concentrating upon one institution at a time and conducting interviews of one to two-and-a-half hours. The number of scheduled interviews conducted with librarians and university administrators in each of the systems ranged from twenty-five to thirty, with a total of eighty-three interviews conducted among the three institutions. The administrative positions the interviewees held varied among the three institutions. In addition to the university librarian or director of libraries, interviews were conducted with all campus library chiefs and with as many library department heads as possible. (During the period of this study, no library system had associate or assistant library directors.) A broad spectrum of university administrators and faculty members were also interviewed.

With the exception of two participants interviewed by telephone, all interviews were held in person. Each session was recorded on a hand-held cassette recorder, with notes frequently taken at the same time. Participants were assured that this study was not judgmental or evaluative but descriptive. It was made clear that the study was being undertaken to learn about organizational processes and problems, not to evaluate people or services, and that anonymity of individuals and institutions would be assured as appropriate. Although none of the participants interviewed requested such anonymity, each was told that responses to the questions would not be reported with individual attribution. Therefore, in the interest of confidentiality, participating institutions and their locations, as well as the individual respondents, are not named; pseudonyms were devised for each institution and its component campuses.

Significance of the Study

While there have been a few surveys of individual multicampus libraries, and one extensive case study of attempts to develop a city multicampus university library system, a review of the literature reveals that there is no scholarly study of multicampus university libraries as a type. Lee and Bowen state that among many important elements of higher education that they did not review were libraries and their management.[47] A comparative analysis of the organization and administration of selected private and public multicampus library systems would contribute to an understanding of some important changes that have occurred in higher education in the last decades. The rapid rise in the number of multicampus university systems, the large number of students involved, and the consequent increase in the complexity of administration and operation of their libraries all suggest the importance of a study such as that reported here.

More immediately, a descriptive analysis of library services provided by multicampus libraries and the recorded observations of autonomy versus consolidation at work, or centralization versus decentralization, should be of interest and, perhaps, of help to library managements facing similar situations, particularly if patterns of cause and effect, problem and solution can be seen. Each of the systems examined ranges from three to six campuses, with sufficient differences in administration and autonomy of campuses and their libraries to present multiple approaches to the organization and administration of multicampus library systems, from autonomous to centrally administered systems. Since there are no two identical situations and institutions, only comparable ones, a comparison of organizational structures found in particular private and semi-public multicampus libraries, while not at all definitive, can be suggestive. This methodology should permit reproducibility and wider application in suggesting hypotheses for future studies.

It should be emphasized this is not an evaluative study of the effectiveness of each library or each library system, nor of the administrative details of operating a library unit. Rather it is an examination of organizational structures, patterns of governance, and key policies in libraries of selected private and semi-public multicampus universities.

Notes

[1] According to the National Center for Educational Statistics, a "university" is an institution that: (a) gives considerable stress to graduate instruction, (b) confers undergraduate and graduate degrees in a variety of liberal arts fields, and (c) has at least two professional schools that are not exclusively technological. U.S. National Center for Educational Statistics, Library Statistics of Colleges and Universities,

1977: Institutional Data (Washington, D.C.: National Center for Educational Statistics, 1980), p. 11.

[2] Eugene C. Lee and Frank M. Bowen, The Multicampus University: A Study of Academic Governance (New York: McGraw-Hill, 1971), p. 1.

[3] Ibid., p. 68.

[4] Edward G. Holley, "Organization and Administration of Urban University Libraries," College & Research Libraries 33 (May 1972): 179. Examples cited by Holley for each category include: (1) branch type campuses--University of Illinois at Chicago Circle, University of Missouri-Kansas City; (2) small colleges that became universities--Georgia State University and University of Wisconsin-Milwaukee; and (3) private universities converted to public institutions--Universities of Buffalo, Houston, Pittsburgh.

[5] Clark Kerr in Lee and Bowen, The Multicampus University, p. xi.

[6] Holley observed: "... urban universities promised to be as significant for twentieth-century urban America as the land-grant college had been for nineteenth-century agricultural America." (Holley, p. 179.)

[7] Enrollment figures in the urban universities of the 1960s indicate marked increase: by 1969/70 urban university enrollment consisted of 19.4% of full-time, 31.8% of part-time, and 22.6% of the total students enrolled in higher education. Garland G. Parker, "Fifty Years of Collegiate Enrollments: 1919-20 to 1969-70," School & Society 98 (Summer 1970): 287.

[8] William M. Birenbaum, Overlive: Power, Poverty and the University (New York: Dell

Publishing Co., 1969), p. 28: "Most of the country's outstanding universities are now urban-based. Those which aren't are reaching out for the nearest city as rapidly as they can ..."

9 Lee and Bowen, The Multicampus University, p. 1.

10 Ibid., p. 2.

11 Ibid.

12 According to Charles D. Churchwell, "The Library in Academia: An Associate Provost's View," in New Dimensions for Academic Library Service, ed. E. J. Josey (Metuchen, N.J.: Scarecrow Press, 1975), p. 22: "Between 1960 and 1970, the student population increased by more than 133 percent, a very sharp rise from almost 3.5 million to more than eight million students."

13 Carnegie Commission on the Future of Higher Education, Less Time, More Options: Education Beyond the High School: A Special Report and Recommendations by the Carnegie Commission on Higher Education (New York: McGraw-Hill, 1971), p. 7.

14 Lee and Bowen describe the advantages of multicampus systems: "... multicampus systems have the advantages of size and the added benefit of a form of governance with potential for variety and change. Even with fewer students and less support, a multicampus system can maintain its effectiveness by pursuing the objectives of campus diversity ..., campus specialization ..., and campus cooperation ..." Eugene C. Lee and Frank M. Bowen, Managing Multicampus Systems: Effective Administration in an Unsteady State (San Francisco: Jossey-Bass Publishers, 1975), p. 4.

15 By the 1970s three-fourths of the students in public universities were enrolled in multicampus university systems. Lee and Bowen, The Multicampus University, pp. xi, xviii.

16 A report issued by the U.S. Office of Education, Library Statistics of Colleges and Universities, 1963-64: Analytic Report (Washington, D.C.: National Center for Educational Statistics, 1968), p. 4, states: "The sharpest increases over the 5-year span (1959/60-1963/64) have occurred in number of volumes annually acquired, and total operating expenditures. The increase per year for the former averaged over 10 percent; for the latter over 15 percent."

17 For example, the Higher Education Facilities Act of 1963 which granted funds for library construction and the Higher Education Act of 1965 which authorized grants for collection growth. According to the National Center for Educational Statistics, "... during the fiscal year ended June 30, 1966, over 1,800 Federal grants were awarded to academic institutions for the purchase of library materials. The total Federal sum was approximately $8.2 million." Ibid., p. 4.

18 This question of centralization or decentralization of academic libraries has been extensively examined in the professional literature, and usually in the context of a single-campus system. Symposia on the subject include: "Centralization or Decentralization of Library Collections: A Symposium," Journal of Academic Librarianship 9 (September 1983): 196-202; "Centralization and Decentralization in Academic Libraries: A Symposium," College & Research Libraries 22 (September 1961): 327-340, 398.

19 J. Michael Bruno, "Decentralization in Academic Libraries," Library Trends 19 (January 1971): 316.

Introduction   25

[20] The conclusions of the Carnegie Commission
can apply to a study of libraries of multicampus universities: "Strong centralization
of authority in multicampus sytems ... can
delay decisions and make them less responsive
to specific problems. Reasonable decentralization to the campus level within multicampus systems ... can accelerate and personal-
ize the making of many decisions." Carnegie
Commission on Higher Education, Governance of
Higher Education: Six Priority Problems (New
York: McGraw-Hill, 1973), p. 15.

[21] "... there are various combinations of
these types of centralization, depending
again upon such factors as historical conditions, personality strengths or weaknesses,
types of library quarters, and the nature of
library operations." Maurice F. Tauber,
"Introduction," in "Centralization and Decentralization in Academic Libraries: A Symposium," p. 327.

[22] "When today's technology is utilized
fully, the issue of centralized collections
will fade into oblivion." Anne Woodsworth,
"Decentralization Is the Best Principle of
Organization Design Where It Fits," in "Centralization or Decentralization of Library
Collections: A Symposium," p. 199.

[23] Lee and Bowen, The Multicampus University,
p. xv. Miller adds: "The simple fact is that
in certain respects higher education has out-
grown its shell--its shell being the independent, single-campus institution." James L.
Miller, Jr., "Coordination Versus Centralized
Control," in The Expanded Campus, ed. Dyckman
W. Vermilye (San Francisco: Jossey-Bass Publishers, 1972), p. 237.

[24] Eugene C. Lee and Frank M. Bowen, The Multicampus University: A Study of Academic Governance (New York: McGraw-Hill, 1971). Clark
Kerr noted that although the rise of the mul-

ticampus institution is one of the most important organizational changes in higher education, the subject is one of almost complete neglect. Clark Kerr in Lee and Bowen, Ibid., p. xi.

[25] Ibid., p. 14.

[26] Ibid., pp. 416-419.

[27] Eugene C. Lee and Frank M. Bowen, Managing Multicampus Systems: Effective Administration in an Unsteady State, A Report for the Carnegie Council on Policy Studies in Higher Education (San Francisco: Jossey-Bass Publishers, 1975).

[28] Peter Sammartino, Multiple Campuses (Rutherford, N.J.: Fairleigh Dickinson University Press, 1964).

[29] Algo D. Henderson and Jean Glidden Henderson, "Interinstitutional Coordination, Multicampus Systems," in Higher Education in America (San Francisco: Jossey-Bass Publishers, 1974), pp. 218-235.

[30] Leonard E. Goodall, "Intercampus Relations in Multicampus Universities," in Crisis in Campus Management: Case Studies in the Administration of Colleges and Universities, ed. George J. Mauer (New York: Praeger Publishers, 1976), pp. 53-68.

[31] Ibid., pp. 56, 58.

[32] Robert C. Keys, "An Analysis of Decision-Making Patterns in Public Multicampus Institutions of Higher Education: An Empirical Model" (Ph.D. dissertation, Arizona State University, 1976).

[33] Sean Van Pallandt, "A Descriptive Study of Systemwide Self-Studies of Multicampus Uni-

Introduction 27

versity Systems" (Ph.D. dissertation, University of Tennessee, 1981).

[34] William Wade Waymer, "A Study of the Actual and Needed Involvement of Central Administrations of Multicampus Systems of Higher Education in the Accrediting Process" (Ph.D. dissertation, Florida State University, 1979).

[35] Patrick Roy Lake, "Common Problems in Organizing and Developing Multicampus Community Colleges" (Ph.D. dissertation, Indiana University, 1979).

[36] John W. Creswell, Ronald W. Roskens, Thomas C. Henry, "A Typology of Multicampus Systems," Journal of Higher Education 56 (January/February 1985): 26-37.

[37] Ibid., p. 35.

[38] William J. Myrick, Jr., Coordination: Concept or Reality? A Study of Libraries in a University System (Metuchen, N.J.: Scarecrow Press, 1975).

[39] Donald L. Ryan, "Libraries in Off-Campus Units," Library Trends 10 (April 1962): 541.

[40] "Report of the Provost's Task Force on University Libraries," Pennsylvania State University, September 18, 1981. (Typewritten).

[41] James G. Neal and Barbara J. Smith, "Library Support of Faculty Research at the Branch Campuses of a Multi-Campus University," Journal of Academic Librarianship 9 (November 1983): 276-280.

[42] John P. McDonald, "The Rutgers University Library: A Study of Current Problems of Organization and Service in a Decentralized University," in Studies in Library Adminis-

trative Problems: Eight Reports from a Seminar in Library Administration (New Brunswick, N.J.: Rutgers University, Graduate School of Library Service, 1960), pp. 95-132.

[43] "Rutgers University Libraries Master Plan," Prepared by the University Master Planning Committee on Libraries, May 1, 1979. (Typewritten).

[44] Pseudonyms are used throughout to protect the anonymity and confidentiality of the institutions and the individuals.

[45] Harry Levinson, Janice Molinari and Andrew G. Spohn, Organizational Diagnosis (Cambridge, Mass.: Harvard University Press, 1972), p. 519.

[46] Ibid., p. 32.

[47] Lee and Bowen in Managing Multicampus Systems state: "By design and not oversight, several important areas of multicampus governance are not dealt with here, despite their obvious importance. Among these are ... libraries ... high on systemwide agendas, they demand specialized treatment," p. xv. Further in their study they repeat: "... we have not reviewed many critical elements of the higher education scene, despite their obvious relevance to multicampus systems: for example ... library management .... These are critical problems now. They will not lessen in the years ahead," Ibid., p. 133.

CHAPTER II

INSTITUTION I (HARRISON UNIVERSITY)

A. <u>THE ENVIRONMENT: THE UNIVERSITY AND ITS
   SETTING</u>

<u>Background and Description</u>

Harrison University is in a major metropolitan area. It has three campuses in a large city and two in nearby suburbs (see figure 1). There are also branches of the university in Rome, Italy and in Tokyo, Japan that offer fine arts and business programs, respectively.

Institution I has a total enrollment of more than 30,000 students and declares in its publications that it is committed to educating disadvantaged students, handicapped students, and those for whom English is a second language. Its mission is stated as:

> ... a multi-purpose public university ... in a major urban center ... [that] carries on a variety of functions, ranging from its historic mission of providing broad access in its undergraduate programs to the more advanced graduate programs, and ranging from a major emphasis on basic research and scholarship to its public usefulness.[1]

In the 1960s through a legislative act Harrison University was designated one of three state-related universities,[2] with

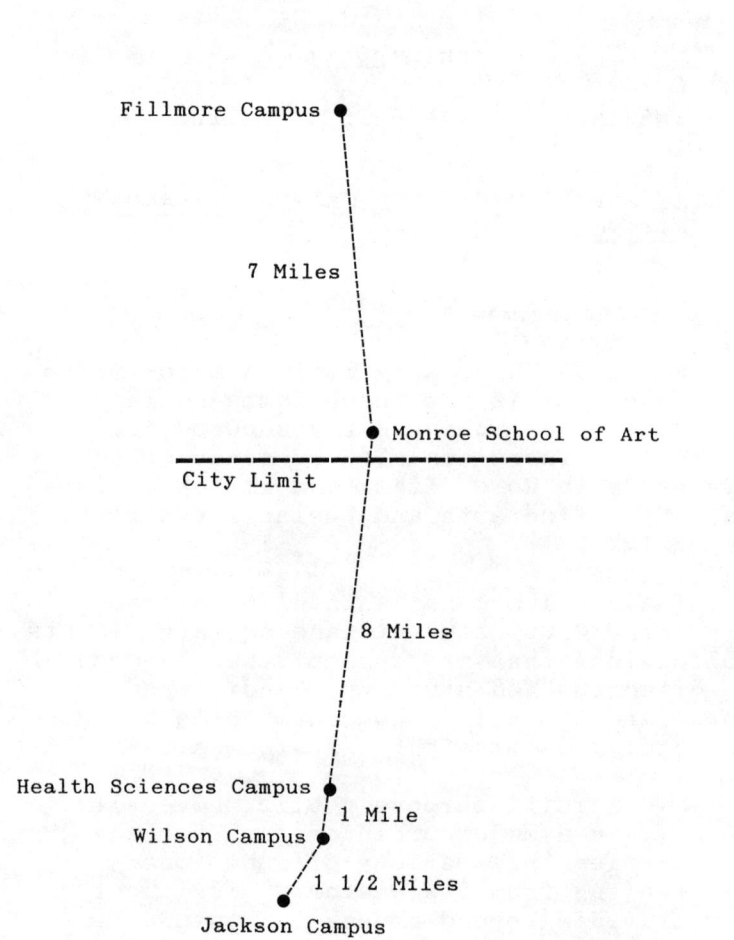

Figure 1
HARRISON UNIVERSITY
DISTANCES BETWEEN CAMPUSES BY AUTO ROUTE

approximately one-third of its funding thereafter coming from the state.[3] As a state-related institution, over 80% of its students are native to the state. Harrison University is governed by a board of trustees, of which one-third are state appointed, four are appointed by the governor of the state, four by the president pro tempore of the state senate, and four by the speaker of the state house of representatives.

The university is comprised of sixteen schools and colleges offering baccalaureate and graduate degrees in more than one hundred fields (of which fifteen are Ed.D.s in education). Professional degrees are offered in law, medicine, dentistry, and pharmacy at separate schools for each, plus degrees from a college of allied health professions. The university operates a major teaching hospital as an adjunct to its medical school. In addition, a university extension office offers continuing education courses to adults at some forty off-campus locations in the state and in Mexico and Puerto Rico. The university's total full-time and part-time faculty number approximately 2500.

The university is more than a hundred years old. In the late 19th century an impecunious deacon in a local Baptist church (which is still located on the original campus) asked the minister for help in studying for the ministry. The minister offered to tutor him and some of his friends. From that group of seven students grew a college. Four years later the student body had grown to 590 and the trustees obtained a state charter of incorporation for a non-sectarian college whose purpose was described as "the support of an educational institution intended primarily for the benefit of workingmen."[4]

The first amendment to the college charter in 1891 extended the purpose to "... the support of an Educational Institution intended primarily for the benefit of Working Men; and for young men and women desirous of attending the same."[5] At the same time the college was granted the right to confer degrees, the first of which was conferred for Bachelor of Oratory, a degree probably never before granted elsewhere in the U.S.

The college grew. The law school opened in 1895, the school of music in 1896, the department of medicine in 1901, the school of pharmacy in 1905. In 1907, as an indication of its arrival as a significant institution of learning, a dental college and a related hospital merged with the college. These institutions, together with another hospital, formed the newly named Harrison University on what is now the health sciences campus located on sixteen acres one mile north of the university's original campus (Wilson campus). By 1922, the university consisted of twelve schools and colleges, approximately 400 faculty (many part-time) and over 8,000 students.[6] In 1935 the first of the multicampuses, an art school, was created on a suburban estate donated to the university (Monroe school of art campus) and in 1958 a forty-eight year old independent horticultural school for women merged into the university to become in time a second attractive and highly successful suburban campus. At first a junior college, this campus changed its name in 1961 to signify its status as a complete campus of the multicampus university (Fillmore campus).

As Harrison University's programs steadily expanded, it became by 1965 what the university provost has described as a "... private university with a strong liberal arts orientation, a history of education in business and management, several professional schools, and a few notable graduate and research programs."[7] The dramatic growth of the

University I (Harrison University)

university is statistically demonstrated by enrollment: in 1947 there were approximately 10,000 full-time and part-time students; in 1975-76 there were 35,000 full-time and part-time students each semester, with approximately 50,000 different students attending throughout the year.[8] Contributing to this growth was the defined role given the university in a 1971 master plan for higher education in the state to limit its lower division enrollment and increase the number of upper-division transfer students, mostly from the new community college systems in the state.[9] It was with the state-related status that the university became a comprehensive university and the university's goals became "... to provide high-quality, low-cost education in virtually every discipline, conduct outstanding research, and perform important public service."[10] The state's master plan was also concerned with coordination among the state universities, with the result that the presidents of the universities were encouraged to explore aspects of coordination at all academic levels and of "... key non-teaching areas such as library, computer and instructional technology."[11]

Harrison University began to expand physically with major growth at the Fillmore campus and the creation in 1973 of a fourth campus in the business center of the city (Jackson campus).[12] The original Wilson campus and the health sciences campus were kept in their present locations in neighborhoods which "... changed very quickly from a white, middle class to a black, working class area in the post-war period."[13] In the 1950s, the administration had considered the merits of "... retreating from the concrete of [the city] to the tree-shaded suburbs. But [the University's] die had been cast long ago, and the decision was made to continue as a part of the urban community."[14] The president stated the decision made by the trustees to stay in the city was, he thought, a wise one. "The problems of urban society are not going to be dealt with away from the city. [The University] will do whatever is in its appropriate orbit to contribute to the improvement of urban life without sacrificing academic excellence."[15] This act of faith is a reflection of the university's commitment to education for all, a commitment dating back to its genesis. When the founder had agreed to teach a young aspiring minister, he laid the groundwork for what is now called the "People's University."[16]

Adhering to the people's university concept, the university has adopted a continuing dedication to its surroundings and environment. This emphasis upon urban issues was recognized by the Middle States Commission of Higher Education evaluation team in their 1977 visit:

> We were particularly impressed by the degree of consensus that the basic goals of [Harrison] University ... must be a people's university, a populist institution, stressing broad access and a willingness to serve its community, but that it can best fulfill this mission within the context of a heterogeneous system of public higher education by stressing quality .... It must remain an institution which ... can be the source of technical assistance to the broad community which it wishes to serve.[17]

The effect upon the surrounding community is considered before any addition to the university's Wilson and health sciences campuses, as, for example, the announcement in November 1985 of the installation of a new supercomputer system. The president stated that the new system "... may also advance efforts by [Harrison University] and its community to attract new industry to the long-

University I (Harrison University)

neglected section of [the city] where [the University's] Wilson campus and Health Sciences Center are located."[18] Successive annual reports of past presidents document many of the community services the university has continued to provide through the years, e.g., a legal aid office operated by the law school, dental clinics and other health care services, and community performing arts programs.

A massive and ambitious long-range plan suggested by the current president is to deal with the neglected area surrounding the two campuses by encouraging the growth of improved local schools, new business and industry, and housing. To accomplish this, he proposes to make the Wilson campus a catalyst for improvement by revitalizing the campus with restaurants, more dormitories to keep students on campus, housing for faculty and staff to keep them also on campus--"and in full cooperation with our neighbors."[19]

Paired with the university's commitment to the economically ravaged surroundings of the Wilson campus and the health sciences campus is the pride that the university has taken in its efforts to increase minority enrollment. With an approximately 18% black student body, the university had in 1973 more black students than either of the state's historically black institutions. Students, reported the then incumbent president, "... come from welfare homes and mansions .... They come to a university that has a Phi Beta Kappa chapter on one hand and special supportive programs to help out those with deficiencies in background and education on the other."[20] The current president plans to institute a bilingual program consistent with his conviction that "... in view of the composition of the population in this hemisphere, our emphasis should be on Spanish."[21]

While the university has a growing percentage of non-traditional students (e.g., older, returning), the composition of the student body is expected to change within the next five to ten years. This will likely result in a higher percentage of international students generated by the university's foreign campuses and a higher percentage of minority students. Due to the special commitment by the university to minority education and given its location in a disadvantaged area of the city, it is anticipated also that the university will be a fertile source of the next generation of minority college faculty.

Organization and Administration of the University

Significant changes have occurred frequently in the organization of the university. Most recently, in 1982, the university acquired a new president (the university's seventh); since his appointment, all the senior officers of the institution are new. As in many institutions, there has been a reconfiguration of the administrative services and the number of vice-presidents greatly reduced. For example, the positions of two vice-presidents in the academic area have been "collapsed" into one position called the provost.[22] Currently reporting to the president are the positions of vice-president for university administration, provost, vice-president for financial affairs and treasurer, vice-president for the health sciences center, and vice-president for development and alumni affairs (see figure 2).

It is the perception of the director of libraries and other high administrators that with the new president and consequent change of personnel has come a new sense of the mission of the university and a renewed commit-

University I (Harrison University)

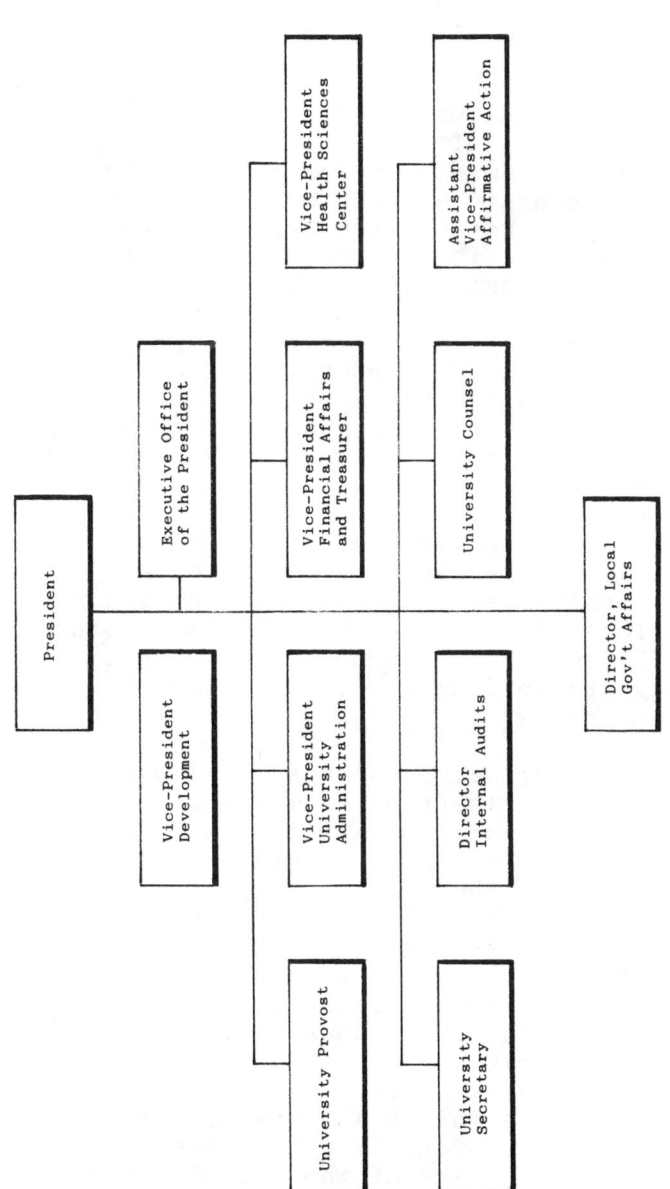

Figure 2
ORGANIZATION CHART: HARRISON UNIVERSITY, OFFICE OF THE PRESIDENT

ment to scholarship. Greater emphasis is being placed on becoming a major "comprehensive" university with strong research orientation.

Harrison University is governed as a flagship system, with the Wilson campus as the center of administration.[23] There was general agreement among interviewees that the other campuses have little true autonomy. From the perspective of the dean of the school of business administration, since the colleges and schools are university-wide, their programs are given on the respective campuses with faculty reporting to a college, not to a campus.[24] It is his position that campuses at the university are simply physical facilities that are managed by people who have the title either of dean or director but who have no academic authority. The Fillmore campus is under a dean, as is the Monroe art school campus. Whereas the other deans of the university are academic deans of schools and colleges that cross campuses, the deans of the Fillmore and Monroe school of art campuses are in charge of their respective campuses only.

All member campuses have equal opportunity to secure resources from the university's central administration. Since two of the campuses have campus deans who sit on the deans' council, they are equally able to argue their cases. (The director of the Jackson campus reports to an associate provost.) In addition, the dean of the Fillmore campus sits on the president's cabinet, an indication of the importance of that position. In the past, various deans of the Fillmore campus have tried without success to turn that campus into a suburban college separate from the university. The present dean, in contrast, is aware of the need for close liaison with the Wilson campus.[25] This awareness is consistent with the policy of the

University I (Harrison University)

current president to place emphasis upon the Wilson campus.

The 1985-86 university budget totaled nearly $250 million (excluding the hospital and the medical school physician's practice plan), with combined state funds providing more than $104 million (41.6%), the annual state appropriation having grown from the original $62 million in 1966/67. As a state-related institution, formal support from appropriations by the state legislature each year provides one-third or more of that year's total operating budget.[26] This is augmented by federal and private grants; student tuition (over $100 million in 1985-86); gifts from alumni, corporations, and friends; and income from endowments. A major source of revenue is tuition. In the recent past the university has experienced an enrollment cycle with consequent fluctuations in tuition generated revenue: a dramatic expansion in the early part of the 1970's after becoming state-related, followed by an enrollment reversal in the late 1970s, in some schools upward of 20%-25%,[27] and by the mid 1980's an increase in enrollment.

A new fund raising program is presently under way to increase endowments. The university continues to place emphasis upon obtaining outside private support through large development campaigns, though it has been state-related since 1965.[28]

The state had assisted the university in earlier times; in 1911 the legislature rescued what was then a college with an appropriation of $110,000.[29] In the 1970s it again became necessary for the state to come to the university's assistance, this time because of its debt-ridden hospital. The hospital, a teaching and research center, had encountered considerable debt because of its services to the needy.[30] The governor and general assembly, upon the advice of a blue-ribbon committee appointed to study the problem, separated the hospital administratively from the health sciences center and created a separate hospital corporation with a fifteen member board of governors wholly responsible to the university's board of trustees.[31] In 1983, with state support and with help from private philanthropy, construction began on a new $129,500,000 hospital complex.

Description of the Campuses

Wilson Campus

The Wilson campus is located on an important artery a short distance from the center of a major city, with an enrollment of more than 14,000 undergraduate and 6,000 graduate and professional school students. The facilities of the campus are located within a twenty-four block area of eighty-two acres with buildings providing administrative offices and classrooms for ten of the university's schools and colleges. These comprise the colleges of arts and sciences; education; engineering and architecture; health, physical education, recreation and dance; and music. Included are the schools of business administration, communications and theatre, law, social administration, and a graduate school.[32] (Many of these offer programs and courses on the other campuses.)

The eclectic architecture of the various buildings ranges from nineteenth century stone Gothic to modern structures and new additions. Current plans include restoration of some of the older stone buildings, row houses and walking areas to the original Federalist design. The concentration of facilities on the Wilson campus ranges from music recital halls and theatres to extensive athletic facilities (in addition to a stadium

University I (Harrison University)

and athletic fields in the northwestern section of the city), residence halls accomodating 1200 students, and university-owned housing complexes. Since the Wilson campus is primarily a commuting campus, there are over a dozen large university parking areas within its boundaries.

The university operates a frequent shuttle bus service to connect the Wilson campus with the other campuses. Students who wish to take classes on more than one of these campuses may use this free bus service. There is no bus service to the Jackson campus as it lies about fifteen minutes from the Wilson campus by subway. Long range planning includes a $5,000,000 subway renovation to move the station stop of the Wilson campus to a more convenient and safer location within the boundaries of the university. The transportation services support the contention of the dean of the Fillmore campus that the entire university can be considered to have a twenty-mile-long campus--the Jackson campus, then the Wilson campus, the health sciences campus, the art school campus, and finally the Fillmore campus.[33]

Monroe School of Art

The Monroe school of art is situated on a fourteen acre campus north of the city. It was established in 1934 on an estate in an elegant and affluent suburban area. The classrooms and painting studios were originally in the main stone house, with the library occupying the dining room and solarium. Studio/classroom buildings and residence halls have been added and in 1974 a much larger library constructed in a new classroom facility. A comprehensive curriculum in the visual arts is offered to some 700 undergraduate and graduate students. Bachelor of fine arts degrees and master of fine arts degrees are offered in five areas--

photography, painting, sculpture, weaving, jewelry--with the opportunity to study for a semester or a year at the branch of the art school in Rome, Italy.

Jackson Campus

The Jackson campus is the downtown campus of the university, located in two remodeled office buildings in the heart of a business district three miles or fifteen minutes by subway from the Wilson campus. It was created in 1973 to provide for the educational needs of adults who live or work in that part of the city. When the campus was launched it was regarded principally as a center for business courses. Now general courses are offered, many the same as those available at the other campuses: undergraduate courses; graduate courses leading to master of arts in history, master of public administration, and master of business administration (MBA) concentrations; plus a spectrum of non-credit continuing education programs.

Dramatic growth of this campus occurred soon after it opened with 500 students enrolled in twenty-three courses. Five years later the president described a Jackson student body of 9,000 and reported that the university was expanding programs by leasing space in two additional buildings. "Together with the growth at [the Fillmore] campus, [Jackson] campus," the president wrote, "represents one of the two major areas of enrollment growth at [Harrison] in the last half decade."[34]

Fillmore Campus

The Fillmore campus, located the greatest distance from the Wilson campus, is situated on 187 acres some distance northwest of the city in a flourishing county. Students

University I (Harrison University)   43

are drawn from five neighboring counties and
from other points in the state, other states,
and some foreign countries. The aim of the
campus is to provide "... undergraduate and
graduate students the advantages of an urban
education in a suburban setting."[35] The former school of horticulture for women that
merged with the university in 1958 functioned
in the beginning as a two-year feeder campus.
By the early 1970s the campus had expanded to
include baccalaureate and graduate degree
programs. It was in 1971 that an active plan
to enlarge and promote the campus was approved by a university planning council.[36] In
the 1971-1972 report of the year's activity,
the president indicated that planning for the
future of the campus was underway, as "ample
academic justification for expansion" was
evident.[37]

As the enrollment continued to increase,
the number of course selections jumped from
224 to nearly 1400. Many of the degree
programs and courses offered on the Wilson
campus are available at the Fillmore campus:
undergraduate and graduate programs in the
day, evening, weekends and summer to more
than 6,000 students in thirty-six fields
during the day and thirteen during the late
afternoon and evening; fifteen master's
degrees in arts and sciences, business, education, pharmacy, and recreation; one doctorate in education and one in pharmaceutics (a
combination of pharmacy and management).
Offered also are master of liberal arts
(MLA); master of arts (MA) in mathematics;
master of education (MEd) in elementary education, psychology of reading, recreation and
leisure studies; and master of public administration (MPA).

The campus has a large business school
enrollment, 750 to 800 graduate business
school students who represent almost 60% of
the entire university's graduate population

of the school of business administration; in addition a little over 35% of the university's undergraduate business majors are enrolled on the campus. MBA degrees are offered in civil and construction engineering technology, computer and information sciences, economics, electrical engineering technology, finance, industrial technology, organization and management, and statistics. The Middle States Commission of Higher Education report of 1977 advised the university to examine the future of this campus:

> [Fillmore] must either become more of a self-contained, semi-autonomous branch campus, or remain clearly an extension campus with the [Wilson] campus exercising academic responsibility .... The choice is a very difficult one ... its outcome will affect not only the character of the [Fillmore] campus but that of the University as a whole.[38]

This problem continues to be discussed.[39] The university provost's Proposed Academic Plan of 1985 includes a proposal to develop special programs at only the Fillmore campus for senior executives and managers in high technology industries, and to establish an entrepreneurial center there. The provost also stated that for many, [Fillmore] was viewed as an alternative to the Wilson campus. However, the current administration is determined that Fillmore campus not become a university alternative to the Wilson campus but complement the Wilson and health sciences campuses.

B. THE UNIVERSITY LIBRARIES: STRUCTURES AND PROCESSES

A Brief History of the Library of [Harrison] University written in 1934 by the assistant librarian notes from the 1896-97

University I (Harrison University)   45

catalog that the first "library room" had
been created to "... become an incentive to
personal research so important to a correct
student life."[40] From these three hundred
books in glass-enclosed shelves, accessible
only by means of a key obtainable from the
dean's office, the library grew to two
thousand volumes in 1900, mainly gifts. The
first librarian was appointed in 1912, and as
the balcony room was no longer adequate, a
new "Annex" was built in 1916 at the cost of
$30,000. In the 1917-18 university catalog,
mention is made of the separate collections
of the law school and medical school in their
own buildings. In the first library annual
report of 1918, the librarian included the
holdings of the law school and medical school
libraries in the total count, 10,800 volumes,
a practice that has continued to the present
day. In 1926 the collection numbered 58,000
volumes, with separate branches of business,
education, and theology. In 1935 the library
moved to a new building with a capacity of
250,000 volumes; here Franklin Delano
Roosevelt was awarded an honorary degree
during the dedication of the library. The
special collections room was opened in 1946,
the beginning of a strong component of the
university libraries. With a gift from an
eponymous donor and state construction funds,
the present Wilson campus library with a
capacity for 1,000,000 volumes was opened in
1966. The university libraries had already
become a member of the Association of Research Libraries in 1962. By 1971 the library had acquired its 1,000,000th book and
in 1972 joined OCLC (Online Computer Library
Center). In 1981 the multicampus university
library system (including the law and medical
libraries) joined the Research Libraries
Group and Network while continuing its membership in OCLC.[41] In 1983-84 the university
ranked approximately 80th in the Association
of Research Libraries (ARL) Index, down from
approximately 60th in 1979-80.

A statement of the mission and goals of the university library system appearing in a report prepared in 1980 declares:

> The mission of the Central Library System of [Harrison] University is to support the educational, research, and information service needs of the University, giving due regard to the role of [the University] as the major state-related institution for higher education serving south-eastern [part of the state]. In pursuit of the fulfillment of this mission, the Central Library System will provide full access to all of its learning resources to members of the university community, foster a spirit of cooperation among various university departments housing learning resources ... and make available, as appropriate and as possible, its resources to the citizens of [the state].[42]

Description of the Campus Libraries

Wilson Campus Library

Each campus and divisional library of the university has its own personality and character, reflecting in its collections the distinct population each serves. The Wilson campus library, on the original campus housing the central administration, serves the major body of students, approximately 20,000. Consequently, the size, approximately 1,900,000 volumes, is greater and the contents more comprehensive than the other campus libraries. Located in a contemporary four-story building situated in the center of the campus along a main mall, it is readily accessible from other buildings. The library is reexamining the physical layout of departments within this building in the face of the

University I (Harrison University)

extensive use of the facility made by students; high in its priorities must be additional stack and storage space. The director of libraries has been given sympathetic support by the university administration and a promise of funding to create an improved facility through either renovation or an addition and to acquire an online catalog to support its automated circulation system.

The Wilson campus library has a special collections department created in 1972. The collections include units that reflect the special urban interests of the community. The Wilson campus library complex also includes several divisional libraries which are administratively part of the Wilson campus library but housed in other buildings: the instructional materials center and school of social administration library in the college of education and the engineering and science libraries.

The instructional materials center was established in 1965 by the college of education to support teacher education programs with instructional resources and services. In July 1982, the library became a branch within the Wilson campus library system. The center consists of a reading room with collections of print and non-print instructional materials, primarily circulating collections of textbooks, juvenile books, curriculum guides, standardized tests, filmstrips, videotapes, overhead transparencies, microcomputer software, and a reference collection. The entire collection numbers over 41,000 items, with emphasis primarily on materials that classroom teachers would use from kindergarten through secondary school. The school of social administration's library, a collection emphasizing social work and social welfare literature, is administratively combined with the instructional materials center.

The college of engineering technology is housed in a nine-story building constructed by the state in 1979. Four- and five-year degree programs are offered in architecture; biomedical, environmental, electrical, mechanical, and civil engineering; and construction technology. The former engineering and architecture library housed within that building has been renamed the engineering and science libraries as a result of a recommendation made in an extensive "Office of Management Studies Public Service Study" conducted by the libraries in 1984.[43] Now that divisional library has responsibility for four graduate libraries--biology, chemistry, physics, and mathematical sciences--and the engineering and architecture library, an undergraduate facility. The positions of coordinator of departmental science libraries and head of the engineering and architecture library were merged into head of the engineering and science libraries in 1984 as part of the recommendation made in the same "Office of Management Studies Public Service Study."

Because of the nature of its collection, the engineering library is non-competitive and non-duplicative with the Wilson campus library. Students in engineering very seldom need to use the Wilson campus library across the street. For the 1600 students in the college, all but twenty-seven credits are taken within the engineering building; therefore, the materials to support these courses are in the engineering library only.

All branches of the Wilson campus library are in buildings within several blocks of the Wilson library. It was these divisional libraries to which the Middle States Report of 1976 referred when they recommended:

University I (Harrison University)

> ... assignment to the University Librarian clear responsibility for all institutional library resources, wherever they are located and in whatever form they are. This responsibility should include that of procurement, processing and preparing for use, and of centrally cataloguing of all materials.[44]

These libraries do now report to the director of libraries and these functions are now centralized.

There are two other library complexes on the Wilson campus and the health sciences campus, both operating independently of the university library system--the law library and the health sciences collections--a common arrangement in university libraries. The law library, located a block away from the Wilson campus library, has always been independent, as the law school's accreditation requires that the library be under the law school and report to the dean of the law school. The law school building which houses the law library dates from 1972 after a disastrous fire completely destroyed not only the previous law building but a large part of the law collection. Cooperative efforts with the previous director of libraries of the university resulted in membership in the Research Libraries Group for the law library. Arrangements for extending use of the LEXIS database to the Wilson campus library are underway.

The medical school library dating from 1911 also maintains an independent status, but one not as firm as that of the law library. The director of the health sciences center libraries currently reports to the provost, although that practice is under review.[45] For a number of years the director of libraries of the university conducted a secondary review of the budget of the health sciences center libraries, but this is no

longer the case. The two libraries of the
health sciences center are the medical school
library and, in a separate building, the dental, allied health, pharmacy library.[46] Each
of the two libraries has its own budget, does
its own ordering, cataloging, and reference.
As they too became members of the Research
Libraries Group at the time the Wilson campus
library became a member, they do their cataloging through RLIN (Research Libraries Information Network). The tapes with RLIN cataloging records of the health sciences and
law libraries are also received by the Wilson
campus library, although nothing has been
done with them up to now. Some tentative
discussion has taken place concerning the
possibility of the law and health sciences
libraries linking into the automated circulation system of the Wilson campus library; the
law librarian sees no advantage to the law
library from participating in the Wilson campus library's automated circulation system.[47]
The Association of Research Libraries (ARL)
statistics, however, do reflect the total
collections of the university as the statistics of both the law library and the medical
center libraries are given to the director of
libraries.

Monroe School of Art Library

The Monroe school of art library in a
self-contained art school campus houses a
collection of art, art history and some general studies materials--altogether over
25,000 volumes, 107 current periodical titles
and 900 microfilms. Since art history
courses are also taught at the Wilson campus,
duplication of the most heavily used art
books for both libraries has become an accepted necessity; reserve titles, in particular, had created a problem before the decision to duplicate titles was made. Special
art collections, such as an extensive collection of slides, a large picture file and

University I (Harrison University)

exhibition catalogs add to the strength of
the art school library.

Located on the first floor of a major
classroom and studio building, the library is
centrally located and accessible to the resident faculty and students. Since all courses
and activities take place in a concentrated
area of the school, the library is a physical
presence closely integrated with the students' scholastic life. The 1968 circulation
of 4,708 has grown to 22,383, partly due to
growth in enrollment but also to improved
library facilities. For library needs other
than the art collection, students have access
to the Wilson and Fillmore campus libraries
via the free university shuttle bus system,
in addition to intercampus library loan requests.

Unique to the art school campus is a
collegial faculty assembly with formal by-laws. An amendment to the by-laws stipulated
that membership, with vote, be extended to
the professional librarian in charge of the
art school library.

Jackson Campus Library

The library at the Jackson campus is not
likely to grow substantially; its collection
is small, some 6,000 to 7,000 volumes. It is
agreed by those concerned that it is impossible to provide on-site library support for
all the courses that are given on the campus,
considering space and financial constraints.
Since it is such a small library, the present
strategy is to concentrate on making it an
access point--that is, to provide speedy service from the Wilson campus library. The new
director of libraries has elected to facilitate this by putting the Jackson campus library under the direction of the access services department of the Wilson campus library, the department which is also in charge

of intercampus and interlibrary loans. The
success of this measure is to be assessed
after a year.

With the installation of an online circulation system in the Jackson campus library to be connected to the Wilson campus circulation system (expected Summer 1986), access to materials in the Wilson campus library will be made readily available. It is the aim of the current director of libraries to focus attention on providing electronic access to Wilson campus holdings, fast retrieval of items from the Wilson campus library, efficient reserve services, increased reading space, and other similar services.[48] A fast delivery system is being established so that a title requested will be delivered the same or next working day. The Jackson library itself would simply provide a core reference collection and a current periodicals collection. The collections of the Jackson library, now not intended for the support of the wide range of courses and curricula of the graduate and undergraduate programs offered on that campus, do provide library services to senior citizens and the general community.

Fillmore Campus Library

The library supports undergraduate and graduate courses with a collection of some 80,000 books, bound periodicals, microfilm, and maps. When the university purchased the school of horticulture in 1958, it inherited a small library of horticultural materials. The horticultural program, available only on the Fillmore campus, is reflected in the library's unique and comprehensive collection of books on horticulture. The undergraduate degree programs and graduate level degree programs in other fields that were initiated in the 1970s require greater library resources but the campus library is at present

University I (Harrison University)   53

limited in floor space. The need for space
in the Fillmore campus library is constantly
addressed in reports. As an example, in 1977
an annual report stated:

> The most pressing need for space is that
> of the library at [the Fillmore campus].
> Here there is a total of approximately
> 8000 sq. ft., barely enough for 50,000
> volumes ... when the nature of the pro-
> grams and the size of enrollment require
> a minimum of 100,000 volumes .... [Fill-
> more] desperately needs a library build-
> ing ... for the student body and bur-
> geoning graduate work now given there.[49]

To alleviate the shortage of space, the dean
of the campus has expressed his commitment to
providing the library additional space in the
building in which it is housed.

The Fillmore campus library is, in some
ways, a miniature of the Wilson campus library, offering all the services that the
Wilson campus library offers. In addition to
books and journals, the library provides
audiovisual support via software and videotapes and a library media center with a collection of records and language tapes, computer literature searching and interlibrary
loans. It is understood that the Fillmore
campus library will never be a research library but will develop a core collection to
support course work. The needs of graduate
students are consequently met by interlibrary
and intercampus library loan or by referral
to specific graduate level collections on the
Wilson campus or to neighboring university
collections. Students may borrow books from
the other university libraries in person or
through the Fillmore campus library; intercampus deliveries are made daily.

Organization, Governance and Administrative Structure of the Libraries

During the past years the administrative structure of the university libraries has undergone a series of structural reorganizations reflecting the parent institution's changes (for the present organization see figure 3). In December 1968 the director of libraries (who had been appointed two years earlier) created two new positions, one, assistant director of technical services, the other, assistant director of public services, an arrangement that continued unchanged until 1980.

In 1980 the library system conducted a self-study of the organization of its multicampus library system under the guidance of the Office of Management Studies of the Association of Research Libraries. As part of the project, librarians from all campuses sat on committees formed to study the structure of library administration and the organization of functions. The directive given was to identify problem areas and offer recommendations.[50] On the basis of the recommendations of that study, the library system was reorganized. The two assistant director positions were dropped and replaced by a single deputy director as second in command who would share the reporting relationships with the director.

After a period of time it was determined that the reporting lines to and job descriptions of the director of libraries and the deputy director were unclear since they were in actuality functioning as "co-equals." During the course of the Office of Management Studies Public Service Study, the director of libraries left the university, the deputy director was appointed acting director, and then left after nine months for another position. A management team of four department

University I (Harrison University)

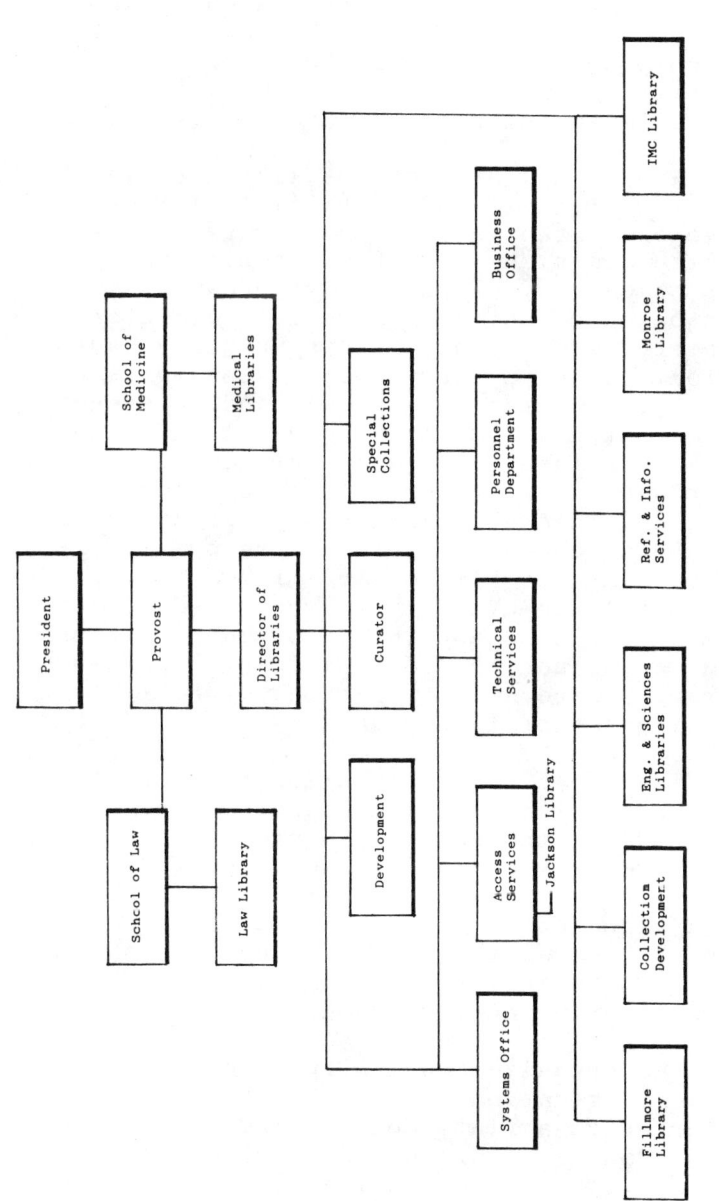

Figure 3
ORGANIZATION CHART: HARRISON UNIVERSITY LIBRARIES

heads was elected by the department heads as an interim governing board during the search for a permanent director.[51] The management team served for almost a full year reporting to the provost[52] and was then retained for the rest of the year by the new director of libraries as an informal advisory group.

With a new director of libraries in place as of April 1985 (the fifth library director in ten years), administrative organization decisions were now again in the process of change. This time, two new positions were being created: an associate director for automated and administrative services (automation, technical services, access services, budget management, personnel) and an associate director for collection development and public services (campus and branch libraries, reference, collections). All department heads and chiefs of all campus libraries are to report to one or the other associate director. At the time of this researcher's interviews, however, the associate directors had not yet been appointed so that department heads at Wilson and the chiefs of the campus libraries were still reporting directly to the director of libraries.

The director of libraries, also referred to as the university librarian, reports to the provost, the chief academic officer of the university community (see figure 4), who in turn reports to the president.[53] (The deans also report to the provost.) Since 1979 the university librarian has sat on the council of deans,[54] although his position is administrative and not faculty.

The organizational structure and internal administration of each of the campus libraries is a flat, centralized model which is not complex. Of the three campus libraries, two are so small as to have no formal organization other than a chief li-

University I (Harrison University)

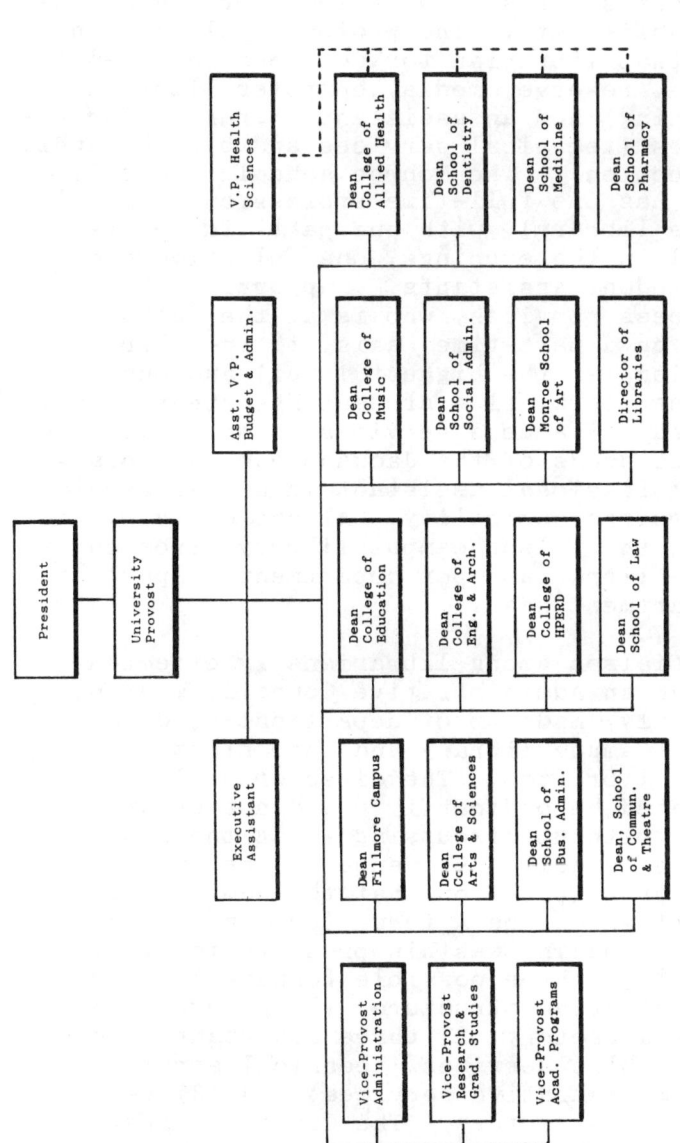

Figure 4
ORGANIZATION CHART: HARRISON UNIVERSITY, OFFICE OF THE UNIVERSITY PROVOST

brarian and a few staff. The Fillmore campus library, the largest of the three, employs in addition to the head of the library, two professionals and six full-time clerks and student assistants. The professionals are an assistant librarian for services (circulation, reserve, media, computer literature searching) and an assistant librarian for resources (technical services and bibliographic instruction). The Monroe school of art library has one full-time professional (chief of the library), with one part-time professional in the evenings, one full-time clerk and student assistants. Supporting the head of access services, who is at the Jackson library on a part-time basis, is one clerical position (at the highest level) and one assistant clerk, plus student assistants. If the head of access services is not available for the needs of the Jackson campus library, her professional assistant in access services assumes responsibility. Almost every librarian in the Wilson campus library (from one to twelve librarians per department) reports to a department head.

Liaison among librarians is effected through an Administrative Council, meeting bi-weekly, made up of department heads of the Wilson campus library and the chiefs of the campus libraries. The director of libraries indicated he ordinarily would not create a policy without discussing it at the Administrative Council. Evidence of the current director's intention that the Administrative Council should be a forum for discussion and decision-making was his presentation to the Council of three possible formats for a new administrative structure: (1) return to a deputy director; (2) three assistant directors: public services, technical services, and administrative services; and (3) two associate directors. The Council's preference (and the director's) was for the third option.[55]

University I (Harrison University)

Administrative policies and procedures can also be developed and implemented by an Academic Assembly of Librarians, a professional body set up in 1970 by the library staff to encompass the entire professional staff and to function on a collegial basis with library administrators. This is the forum to which the director of libraries communicates major issues at bi-monthly meetings, and in which he has expressed a willingness to meet on any policy issue the Assembly would wish to discuss. (He additionally reports monthly to its steering committee.) The responsibilities of the Assembly include maintaining committees on hiring of librarians and on promotion and regular appointment (tenure or continued appointment). The committees make recommendations to the director who has the authority to accept or reject them.

A faculty senate library committee maintains an interest in library policy. While it has not functioned since the new director's appointment, it is expected that any significant policy relating to library performance would be brought to them for discussion in the future. As for the director's relationship with the provost, to whom he reports, he stated that since the provost gives him a great deal of freedom, he tends to keep her informed through regular meetings with the vice-provost and occasional meetings with the provost.[56]

The director of libraries finds the current balance between centralization and local campus authority shifting in the direction of centralization. The libraries have been encouraged to operate together as a system. The fact that all technical services including ordering, cataloging, processing, and all personnel procedures are performed centrally at the Wilson campus library for the campus

libraries as well as for the departmental
libraries[57] contributes to the feeling of a
system. In addition, interlibrary loans and
periodical and continuation subscriptions are
fufilled centrally by the Wilson campus library.

However, both the Monroe school of art
library and the Fillmore campus library regard themselves to a large extent as autonomous although their chiefs report to the
university librarian. Much of this feeling
of independence seems to be the psychological
result of distance, which creates an illusion
of greater autonomy. The director of libraries has observed that although all the libraries are operated as a system, the librarians at the individual campuses tend to identify with each other rather than with the
department heads at the Wilson campus. In
his view this is a defensive alliance by
those who feel disadvantaged by their distance from the Wilson campus library. In a
strict reporting sense, however, their independence is considered to be no greater than
that of the engineering library located
across the street from the Wilson campus
library.

Even though the director of libraries'
philosophy embraces centralization, there is
a degree of autonomy of each campus library
in the fact that each has its own budget to
administer.[58] Therefore, unless there is a
need for money, staff or services from the
central library administration, the libraries
in fact function fairly independently in day-to-day decision-making within each department
and each campus. When problems surface that
may affect the entire library system, decisions and policy are laid down on the broader
level by the director of libraries. In the
view of the personnel officer of the library,
the actual extent of day-to-day control that
the new director of libraries exercises is

University I (Harrison University)

not clear yet and is being established now, cordially. The new director of libraries has expressed his intention to advocate as few decisions as possible at the central level, but rather attempt to push decision-making downward in the organization. He has stated his belief in delegation of authority and responsibility so long as university-wide policies such as those for circulation and fines for the online circulation system are consistent.

Relationships among the libraries are harmonious. The chief of the Fillmore campus library, who would most likely feel tension should it exist, has emphatically stated that everyone cooperates and is willing to share. This in spite of the geographical locations, a consideration for the chiefs of the campus libraries since because of the distances they are not available for all meetings. Nevertheless tension, if it occurs, appears to be minimal; differences seem to be settled in the Administrative Council, where a high degree of cooperation is displayed.[59]

Libraries have been involved in planning on a coordinated and cooperative system-wide basis. In September 1984 a year-long self-study of public services delivered by the university libraries was completed.[60] Over one hundred recommendations were submitted by the nine member study team and four specialized task forces comprised of twenty-four library staff members.[61] The new director of libraries is examining and addressing each of the recommendations.

Currently, planning evolves through existing committees. An Automation Planning Committee and an Automation Implementation Committee, both with representives from the campus libraries, cooperated in developing an online circulation system and in planning for the online catalog. In addition to working closely with the Automation Planning Committee, the director of libraries has appointed a system-wide budget task force to advise him. After reviewing the Association of Research Libraries "OMS Recommendations" for additional system-wide standing committees in various areas of public services, he has proposed to the Administrative Council the establishment of three such committees: collection development, processing services, and public services. The director concedes that library standards and operating procedures as a whole are not uniform. This is a reflection of his belief in a moderate approach, by which a library should have only a few policies and should encourage staff to be flexible and creative in achieving the goals of the organization; he is more concerned with service to patrons.

The relationship between campus librarians and campus academic departments varies campus to campus. The head of the college of engineering and science libraries, for example, finds a collegial environment in the college of engineering and participates in such college of engineering committees as an educational media resources committee. This close relationship is further cemented by the practice of the college of engineering to pay for all audiovisual equipment and for a recently acquired IBM computer and printer in the library. The librarian also works closely with the faculty in the selection of journals for all the science libraries.

On the Fillmore campus communications with faculty are weak. Since the faculty is part-time and not in residence, little opportunity exists for the library to be proactive and, for example, to approach departments and faculty for suggestions for materials. Currently the only formal meeting with faculty would be at the faculty senate meetings held once a month at the Wilson campus and con-

University I (Harrison University)

nected with the Fillmore campus through an intercom system.

At the Monroe school of art campus, because the faculty is a resident faculty, an informal and close relationship could be established more easily between the chief of the library and faculty and department chairpersons. This is evidenced by the fact that the library head is a voting member of the local faculty assembly and has served as chairperson.

The acting head of the instructional materials center and school of social administration library meets with a faculty library committee of the school of social administration three to four times each year to discuss library matters. He hopes to develop a similar advisory committee in the college of education after a new dean of the college has been appointed.

The director of libraries described the relationship of the chief of each campus library to the campus administrative officer as informal but cordial and excellent. This description includes his own association with the deans or directors of those campuses--cooperative relationships.[62] The chief of the Fillmore campus library finds that her relationship with the dean of the campus is one of information-giving. This includes sending copies of all major reports and discussing with him such plans as the possible development of an information brokerage service at the Fillmore campus library. She would like to meet with him on a more regular basis, as well as with the faculty. The chief of the Monroe school of art library is aware of the importance of communication with the dean of the campus. That dean holds regular meetings with the staff and has invited the head of the library to participate as a member. The head of access services of the Wilson campus library has recently assumed responsibility for the Jackson campus library and is uncertain at this time about the degree of independence of that library and exactly where the library fits into the Jackson campus structure.[63]

Without exception the opinions expressed by the director of libraries, chiefs of campus libraries, and deans of the campuses left no doubt that the primary responsibility of the campus library chief is to the director of libraries. The response of the head of access services (with responsibility for Jackson library) is pertinent: "What really establishes the lines of administrative authority is the budget. Since the budget comes out of the central library system, the director of libraries has the ultimate power."[64] But at the same time as they report to the director of libraries, the chiefs of the campus libraries voiced a strong sense of responsibility to the dean or director of their campuses. As an example, library hours for holidays are discussed with the campus dean or director, as well as security issues, physical plant problems, responsibility for moving to other quarters, furniture, stacks. Space problems, in particular, constitute a major responsibility of the director or dean of a campus and are a point of frequent discussion between the chief of a campus library and the campus administrator. The head of access services stated that as far as space problems are concerned, it really is not up to the director of libraries "to fight for space, but, rather, it's more the head of the particular library and the dean of the campus to figure out where to get the space."[65] Most recently at an Administrative Council meeting, the chief of the Fillmore campus library announced that definite commitments had been made for additional space and that it had been dealt with outside the central library system.

University I (Harrison University)   65

     While in the past major changes in cam-
pus library procedures had been discussed by
the director of libraries with the local campus administrator, the decision to convert
the Jackson campus library into an access
point to the Wilson campus library and not
attempt to purchase materials to support the
degrees offered at Jackson was made by the
director of libraries without consultation
with the new director of Jackson campus.
That there would no longer be a librarian
present at all times to provide reference
service was not viewed favorably by the
director of the campus who was told that via
telephone, reference service could conveniently be provided by the nearby Wilson campus library.

     The director of libraries indicated that
local policies for purchasing materials and
equipment are made within the framework of
system-wide policies or university priorities, as well as the program needs of the
individual campuses, though he is not certain
whether current results reflect this. At
this time each campus makes its own decisions
about the materials it wants to buy, with a
priority for materials set within the individual libraries. The situation is different
for equipment purchases, however. Since the
university is now emerging from a period of
financial constraints during which little
equipment was purchased, the demand is so
great for new and replacement equipment that
the director of libraries feels there is
almost no need to be concerned about priorities.[66]

Collection Development

     The director of libraries has taken the
initiative in creating a new and potentially
strong department of collection development,
whereas heretofore the head of collection

development had no professional staff reporting to that position. The plan now is to assign several full-time bibliographers in the Wilson campus library to broad subject areas to do selection and collection maintenance with the objective of creating a strong research library collection. A collection of greater breadth and depth was not possible until a one-time supplement of $1,000,000 to the 1985-86 library budget was announced by the provost. The acting head of collection development pointed out that with so much of the monies of the previous budgets allocated to approval plans, periodicals, and continuations, the result was a fairly narrow area of flexibility. Departments within the Wilson campus library also have received allocations from the director after consultation with the head of collection development. The reference department, for example, has a reference collection development committee which apportions the department's allocation among its units (i.e., documents, business, maps.)

An important element in the library's collection development plans for the next several years will be the establishment of a collection development policy for the bibliographers. In the past allocation of funds was based upon historical precedent "that has ebbed and flowed with inflation and budget increases and cuts."[67] The problem had been further compounded when increases or decreases in discretionary budget funds were made categorically by percentages rather than need. Now that fiscal restrictions have been eased and additional monies are available, the acting head of collection development and the director of libraries recognize the need to reexamine programs, student enrollment, number of research faculty, and university priorities in general while maintaining a balance in campus needs.

University I (Harrison University)

Traditionally, campus libraries have had their own line item budgets that have been established by the university director of libraries. At campus libraries requests are initiated by the chief of the individual library based upon budget and the need to support the curricula. Campus libraries tend to acquire what they need most in their collections and borrow what they do not have. In developing their collections, consideration is given to programs that have a high priority and the type of programs served, as well as the differing costs of materials. The bibliographers and campus librarians receive a fair amount of requests for materials from various faculty and departments, with priority given to ordering whatever faculty and graduate students request, especially since research interest can change dramatically and quickly.

No coordinated collection development policy document exists at present. In September 1979 an inter-office communication from the director of libraries announced an ad hoc committee to develop a comprehensive collection development policy for the library system. In the charge to the committee, he referred to the fact that the campus and departmental libraries have "both jointly and individually, special and somewhat unique needs which must be recognized."[68] This charge was never fulfilled, although collection development policies have been written by some campus and departmental libraries.[69] The present director of libraries believes that a coordinated written policy is necessary and plans to assign the project to someone.

Duplication is avoided when possible. The acting head of the instructional materials center is the education bibliographer for the Wilson campus library and thus can minimize duplication in education; the head of the engineering and science libraries is the science bibliographer for the Wilson campus library. The question of distances between campuses becomes a valid consideration when making hard decisions concerning duplication in a multicampus institution, e.g., how frequent is the delivery of intercampus loans and how accessible to students or faculty is the material located in a distant campus library.

The method by which library resources are considered in the university's preparation of specific new program proposals or reviews of existing programs varies. It is the opinion of the director of libraries that the library is ill-advised to decide on its own what the university's priorities are, but must confer with deans and the provost to determine what areas are important. Changes in curricula are approved in the faculty senate, of which the director of libraries is a member, as is a representative of the Academic Assembly of Librarians. The director sits also on the council of deans and the graduate board where program changes are discussed. The libraries have, in spite of such representation, often reacted after the event when changes in curricula have taken place. The subject bibliographers have frequently complained that they find out suddenly about a new doctoral program for which library resources are inadequate. The director of libraries has not been in the university long enough to have been involved in the program process directly, but he does suspect that in the past inadequate library facilities or resources would not have stood in the way of approval of a program.[70] This impression is further conveyed by the head of reference who observed that there has been little recognition of the importance of involving the library at the early stages of curricular planning and that the library historically has never been centrally involved in campus-wide

University I (Harrison University) 69

planning even though accreditation committees for schools or programs seeking accreditation require library information regarding materials and journals in the classifications that relate to the new programs. If appropriate and available, discretionary funds are allocated by the library to the bibliographer for such new material, yet new programs have not brought special allocations in library budgets until this year.

Although libraries have not been considered sufficiently in planning for specific programs, the university library system is an important component of the current university academic plan. The <u>Proposed Academic Plan</u> submitted by the provost to the president in October 1985 sets specific goals for the library system. The report reflects the suggestions made in a document which the director of libraries submitted to the provost in August 1985.[71] One of the priorities set by the provost for the university in the <u>Academic Plan</u> is "a library system suited to its special research and teaching needs."[72] Another goal was to reach the 50th position in ARL rankings by 1990.[73] The provost acknowledged in the report that the libraries' collections have not been maintained in recent years at a level appropriate to a comprehensive research university, so that the library has dropped in rank from the sixth to the eighth decile in the Association of Research Libraries Index.

Among the provost's other recommendations were the creation of an online catalog system linking all the campuses to the automated circulation system at the Wilson campus library, and enlargement of the Fillmore campus library.[74] Interviews with members of the library staff indicate that this is a unique time in the history of the university's libraries as the provost and the president of the university recognize as never before the importance of the library system in their planning.

Personnel Policies

Professional librarians are members of the faculty union and as a result of unionization, personnel and employment policies conform to standards that are uniform throughout the university library system. An exception is the matter of staff development, for which no clear policy exists. There are a few positions held by professional librarians which for university purposes are considered administrative rather than librarian. These positions are not represented by the faculty union; the assistant to the director, for example, is technically an administrator, although a librarian. The systems librarian also is not in the union, nor is the personnel officer of the library. The director of libraries is attempting through the Academic Assembly of Librarians to heal the division between the library administration and the librarians that developed about four years ago when the new faculty union contract took additional administrators (thirteen department heads) out of the union and deemed them administration. The grievance process is uniform for all, as is tuition assistance. Travel funds are not covered by a union contract, but the director of libraries has established a uniform policy to cover that need for professional librarians.[75] Since the clerical employees belong to a different union than the librarians, they are governed by a different system for promotion, salary and benefits.

Examples exist of movement of librarians from a position in one library to another within the system, though librarians must bid for the position when it is posted; the current chief of the Fillmore campus library had been head of the instructional materials cen-

University I (Harrison University)

ter, the acting head of collection development had been chief of the Jackson library, and the head of engineering and science libraries had been head of the mathematical sciences library.

Library Budget Process

The current ratio of total library expenditures to the total institutional expenditures was estimated to be 3% for 1985-86 in comparison with 2.4% in 1984-85, a rise reflecting a substantial increase in library allocations.[76]

Excluding law and medicine, a single budget is developed for the entire multicampus library system. The 1985-86 line item budget for compensation and materials lists individually the 1984-85 actual expended, 1984-85 annual budget, and 1985-86 budgeted amounts for each library (Wilson library, Monroe school of art library, engineering technology library, Fillmore campus library, Jackson library, and instructional materials center). This concludes with a grand total line item budget of over $6 million for all libraries.[77]

A high degree of autonomy exists for expenditures. Once a budget is assigned, a campus library or department exercises unilateral control. Although the degree of control has varied over the years, the ultimate constraint has been the budget allocated that year; within that constraint one could move monies from line to line.

The librarians as yet have not gone through a budget process with the new director of libraries. The director plans to change that as he thinks that budget formation has become too centralized. Nevertheless, he plans to retain ultimate responsibility for the total library budget and in

that sense views it as a centralized budget,
albeit to be created by consensus.[78] As currently planned, each campus library and department will be provided with a financial
analysis illustrating by percentages where
the library system spent its previous budget
(i.e., personnel, books, equipment, supplies,
travel). The analysis will be accompanied by
a comparison of such expenditures by other
ARL libraries, germane now that the university has given the library a mandate to
achieve 50th place in the national ARL
statistics. At the same time, the libraries
will be asked how a budget cut of 10% could
be realized and conversely, where an increase
of 10% should be applied. This process will
involve departments, the Academic Council,
the faculty senate library committee, and
faculty, and will require discussions with
the provost. The end product will be a
system-wide document that will serve both as
a formal budget request and a statement of
the libraries' goals and objectives.[79]

This new procedure for planning, developing, and administering the annual budget
will be supervised by a new budget planning
task force, an advisory body made up of staff
members, librarians, department heads, the
library personnel officer, and the director
of libraries, reflecting the director's
deliberate effort to involve many people in
the budget process. To improve the libraries, the provost announced a major, one-time
supplement of $1,000,000 in the library budget. The director of libraries, in addition,
anticipates an internal reallocation of
$150,000 over the next year or two. Since
the university library system spends a
greater percentage of its total budget on
salaries and personnel than other ARL libraries, the director's goal is to reduce the
salary component as people retire or positions become available and to apply that
money for library materials.[80] The new direc-

University I (Harrison University) 73

tor has been told he has flexibility in budget implementation, so that the libraries have authority to use unexpended salary monies for other purposes.

Cooperation and Resource Sharing

The university library system has been a member of the Research Libraries Group since 1981.[81] The benefits of this membership are promoted in various university publications. For example, the school of business administration brochure for its Ph.D. program in business administration describes the Research Libraries Group and states: "The RLG partnership gives students and faculty at [Harrison] University greater access to the more than fifty million volumes owned by the members of the group." It adds, "Interlibrary loan requests from [Harrison] University receive priority consideration at RLG member libraries, and restricted materials which are not ordinarily available via interlibrary loans may be borrowed."[82] As members of RLG, the campus libraries check their computers for the collections of neighboring universities who are also members; university students with an ID are permitted to use any RLG library's resources. Since RLG libraries give each other priority in interlibrary loan and share without fees, all campus libraries as well as the Wilson campus library enjoy the benefits of the system.

As a member of the Research Libraries Group, the university library places collection development emphasis on two selected areas for RLG, one of them a major one. In addition to RLG membership the university has maintained its OCLC association for interlibrary loan transactions. Earlier in the 1960s, the library system became a member of the Center for Research Libraries, and although occasional references have been made in various annual reports to the expense of such membership, it has remained a valuable source for unique items.[83]

Some minor coordination of services with other libraries in geographic or regional networks takes place; for the most part the coordination is informal and casual. The art librarians in the area maintain a chapter of Art Libraries Society/North America (ARLIS) which provides an informal basis of cooperation in calling upon one another for the answer to a reference question. The special collections librarians in the region meet and work together occasionally, and local area library directors have a luncheon meeting every two to three months. The initiative to form this local group of directors of research libraries was taken in 1969 by the Harrison University library director as a vehicle for discussion of common problems and for building collections and possibly allocating responsibility for purchasing expensive sets coming on the market which need not be purchased by all. While this group still meets, collection building is no longer a major topic for discussion. The attempt at cooperative purchasing with other university libraries in the early 1970s was unsuccessful, possibly because most of the large purchases were duplicated anyway.

In the 1982 "Collection Development Policy Statement" of the Jackson campus library, students are referred to specific university libraries and to libraries outside the university library system to supplement the university libraries.[84] Another form of cooperation is exercised by the chief of the Fillmore campus library with the community college libraries and university libraries nearby; Fillmore students who do not find materials in their own library have access to a variety of libraries in the local area, an option which is frequently more convenient

University I (Harrison University)

and preferable to going to the Wilson campus library in the city.

Nevertheless, intercampus loan activity among the libraries is extensive. Although the Fillmore campus library requests many photocopies of journal articles since its journal collection is fairly small, the Wilson campus library currently borrows more books from the Fillmore campus library than the Fillmore library borrows from the Wilson library; this is expected to change as soon as each campus is part of an online circulation and catalog system. Currently the RLIN (Research Libraries Information Network) computer terminals in each library are used to determine the location of desired titles in Harrison campus libraries. The 1984-1985 annual report of the access services department, which has responsibility for intercampus and interlibrary loans, reported that campus and branch use of Wilson campus library materials has increased 30% over the last two years.[85]

There are examples of planned cross campus resource sharing. The college of engineering offers a few engineering courses at the Fillmore campus and several architecture courses at Jackson campus. To support those courses, the engineering library sends materials for reserve to Fillmore and Jackson libraries. If the material required is found only in a library outside the university, an interlibrary request is routed to the Wilson campus library.

Although the medical library is not part of the university library system, intralibrary loan activity is frequent. Loans obtained from the Wilson library (from the science libraries, in particular) in 1984-85 totalled 394, while the number lent to the Wilson campus libraries was 312, a fairly even exchange.

With the exception of the law library, which restricts access to law students and to those with proper identification and formal requests from their faculty, all university libraries are open to the entire university community. No ID is required for admission to the Wilson campus library from 8-5 daily; after 5 p.m. an ID is required.

Technical Services and Automation

All of the libraries at Harrison University are users of RLIN, and all technical services (acquisitions, cataloging, processing, binding) are done centrally in the Wilson campus library through RLIN (except for the law and the health sciences libraries which do their own inputting in RLIN). Currently the RLIN acquisitions system is being used in the Wilson library although the decision to use the system has been reversed at least three times during past years. It may shortly be reversed again after the new director of libraries evaluates it.

Only the Wilson campus library is currently using the Geac automated circulation system, but the other libraries, divisional and campus, will participate soon. An electronic local area networking system is now being installed to integrate all online systems on the Wilson campus and to link all campuses with the university telecommunications network. The new director of libraries has made the decision to develop a Geac online catalog with Geac acquisitions and serials control in the near future. The report of the director of libraries to the Administrative Council declares: "... progress on the online catalog will also be [a priority] in the 1985/86 budget."[86] The university's vice-provost has also indicated her commitment to it, as has the provost in her Proposed Academic Plan.[87]

University I (Harrison University)

All planning for automation is done centrally and has been carried out by the Automation Planning Committee since 1981. Since it was necessary to arrive at uniform circulation policies for the online system, the actual working out of the plans was done by the Implementation Committee, with representatives from every library establishing material types, loan periods, fines, etc. The head of access services has the responsibility to see that the automated circulation system is extended to all branches and campuses and has developed a time schedule of installations which was presented to the Administrative Council.[88]

Summary

Harrison University (Institution I) was founded in 1884 as "... an educational institution intended primarily for the benefit of workingmen."[89] In its evolvement as a comprehensive university through an era of social and economic change, it maintained the essence of that mission, adding to it a commitment to its local environment, so that today it is regarded as a populist "people's university" with a dedication to urban issues and service to the community. The university will probably be educating a growing number of international and minority students in the foreseeable future, as well as becoming a significant source of minority Ph.D's as faculty for other universities. Without diminishing its historical role as a people's university, it has recommitted itself to scholarship, directing new energies to becoming a comprehensive university with strong research orientation. In the past, this dual purpose has strained its resources as the two goals have competed for scarce dollars.

Harrison University has enjoyed steady growth. It contains today sixteen schools and colleges, offering baccalaureate and graduate degrees in more than 100 fields on five campuses (including the health sciences campus) to approximately 30,000 students, perhaps 80% of whom are native to the state in which the university is located.

Its governance is centralized with the Wilson campus administratively the flagship campus. This form of organizational structure extends to the three campus libraries, with most of the university's library resources concentrated in the Wilson campus library and administrative direction emanating from there.

The campus libraries, each with its own chief librarian, maintain a degree of autonomy, principally in the administration of their respective budgets and in day-to-day decision-making. This is compatible with the stated philosophy of the new university librarian of delegating authority and responsibility downward, leaving intact the establishment of broad system policies at the university librarian level.

Harrison University has undergone frequent organizational changes. Its current president, the seventh, has brought a turnover in all senior officers. In the university library system, the director of libraries, appointed in 1985, is the fifth in ten years. He is initiating new organizational changes, moving toward greater automation and encouraging the campus libraries to operate together as a system.

"History is ever present in the university's goals and mission statement. It is always there - a university that has served people who were working and could not get the conventional education."[90] The development of the people's university concept has been significant to the development of the library collections. It has been recognized that the libraries have to serve as greater resource centers when students are not able to purchase as many books as at other institutions. The student body has a high percentage of first-generation college students, with many from the blue collar working class. This large and important constituency is reflected in the library's collections emphasizing urban civilization and urban studies. The collections also record the kind of institution it has been in the past, as in the fine collections in religion and philosophy, a result of the university's origin as a Baptist college.

Divisional libraries were added to the library system to solve departmental problems. The science libraries had been developed by their particular departments (i.e., chemistry, biology, physics, mathematical sciences). When in the late 1960s they realized they were growing too rapidly to be maintained without professional assistance, they negotiated with the Wilson campus library to enter the system. This added to the diffusion of collections and the increased need to avoid, for financial reasons, holdings duplication.

Duplication of titles in a multicampus institution is related to the question of distances between the campuses. If, for example, Fillmore campus were a little further out, its library would require a more comprehensive collection since students would not have ready access to the Wilson campus library. In the words of the Fillmore library director, "distance really makes a difference in a multicampus university as to whether you are going to be a satellite and depend upon the Wilson campus library, or whether you really need to be supportive of the programs offered at the campus."[91] An ever present problem is financial--getting enough money in the book budget to maintain adequate collections on each of the campuses--a problem common to many multicampus libraries. The university has been a member of ARL since 1962 and had been ranked in the sixth decile in the ARL's Index. It has now dropped some twenty points to the eighth decile, prompting a one-time allocation of an additional $1,000,000 to the library budget for improving the libraries' collections to a level commensurate with a comprehensive research institution and for increasing the general collections of the other campus libraries.

Notes

[1] Report to the Commission on Higher Education Middle States Association of Colleges and Schools. The [Harrison] University Self Study 1977, p. 2-2.

[2] The enabling legislation recorded that it recognized the university "... as an integral part of a system of higher education ... and that it is desirable and in the public interest to perpetuate and extend the relationship between the [state] and [Harrison] University for the purpose of improving and strengthening higher education by designating [Harrison] University as a State-related university." Annual Report of the President 73-74, p. 7.

[3] Self Study 1977, p. 3-1. Some of the benefits of the state-related status listed in the Self Study: "The reduction of tuition, generous appropriations for campus expansion, the means for new colleges and programs, and the building of an exceptional faculty have been some of the gains."

University I (Harrison University)

[4] *Walk 100 Years in a Hundred Feet: The [Harrison] Centennial, An Illustrated Guide to the History of [Harrison] University*, September 1984, p. 4.

[5] Ibid., p. 5.

[6] Ibid., p. 10.

[7] *Proposed Academic Plan, _____, Provost, Submitted to President _____*, October 1985, p. 3.

[8] *Self Study 1977*, p. 4-2. The return of the veterans from World War II "set the stage for the explosive growth era that has only just abated. The GI Bill, the baby boom, the expanding economy, the strong national belief in a college education ... were the major factors supporting such growth." Ibid., p. 4-1.

[9] Ibid., p. 4-4.

[10] *Proposed Academic Plan*, p. 3.

[11] *Report of the President 1971-1972, The Impact of Austerity, [Harrison] University*, p. 16.

[12] New construction can be seen on all campuses. The president in his 1974-1975 annual report was able to announce that in the fifteen years, the state, through the General State Authority, had spent more than $107 million in capital construction projects at the campuses. *[Harrison] ... Being An Annual Report of the President of the University for 1974-1975*, p. 4.

[13] *Self Study 1977*, p. 3-15.

[14] *Report of the President 1969-1970 [Harrison] University*, p. 10.

15 Ibid., p. 12.

16 "The great among humanity," [the founder] declared in a sermon near the end of the century, "are not to be found in fashionable suburbs or in palatial mansions, but amoung (sic) men of low estate." [Harrison] ... Being An Annual Report of the President of the University for 1974-1975, p. 3.

17 Annual Report of the President of [Harrison] University 1976-1977, p. 1.

18 "[Harrison] Update," November 20, 1985. "Harrison's New Supercomputer System Will Advance Research Industry," Office of University Relations. (Typewritten.) Plans include construction on the Wilson campus of a $25 million corporate computer center as part of a planned High-Tech Industrial Park. Ibid.

19 [Harrison] University Report of the President, July 1, 1982-December 31, 1983, p. 7.

20 Annual Report of the President 73-74, p. 9.

21 [Harrison] University Report of the President July 1, 1982-December 31, 1983, p. 25. "The president of [Harrison] University, situated in a black and Hispanic neighborhood in [city] wants to make Spanish a requirement for graduation by 1990 .... 'There are 250,000 Hispanics in the immediate... vicinity, and there will be 30 million in the country by the year 2000.'" "College Head Asks Study of Spanish Be Required," _____, 18 January 1986, p. 6.

22 Interview with the dean of the school of business administration, December 11, 1985. As a result of this new position, according to the dean, there now is an academic plan.

University I (Harrison University)

As observed in other institutions, positions and titles are never static; this has been especially true of the position of the vice-president of academic affairs or its equivalent. Since 1969 the position, its title, its responsibilities have changed several times.

[23] This is seen as part of the president's plan to emphasize the Wilson campus and not overextend into outlying campuses. Interview with the acting head of collection development, October 18, 1985.

[24] "It is the colleges that have the autonomy in the assignment of faculty and the determination of programs. I must approve all teaching schedules, and I must determine where programs are going to be located." Interview with the dean of the school of business administration, December 11, 1985.

[25] Interview with the chief of the Fillmore campus library, January 6, 1986. The current dean of that campus stated emphatically that the campus does not have autonomy. Interview with the dean of the Fillmore campus, January 6, 1986.

[26] Report of the President 1978-79 [Harrison] University, p. 4.

[27] Interview with the vice-provost, November 21, 1985.

[28] In his 1978-79 annual report, the president stated: "The mixture of private and public funding enriches an institution and provides for a vigorous interchange of ideas and philosophies." Report of the President 1978-79 [Harrison] University, p. 5.

[29] [Harrison] ... Being An Annual Report of the President of the University for 1974-1975, p. 4.

[30] The university hospital had accumulated a deficit of $25,000,000, "... incurred by providing free or subsidized services to ... neighbors ..." Self Study 1977, p. 3-9.

[31] A statute was enacted on October 8, 1975 which authorized the state to acquire the hospital for $30,000,000 with the proviso that it be leased back to the university to operate. The university then used the $30,000,000 to pay off the accumulated debt. Annual Report of the President of [Harrison] University for 1975-76, p. 9.

[32] The only programs not available on the Wilson campus are those offered by the department of horticulture and landscape design, college of allied health professions, and the schools of dental hygiene, dentistry, medicine, pharmacy, and art.

[33] Interview with the dean of the Fillmore campus, January 6, 1986. He has stated that it is very useful to think of the university as a single corridor tied together by a fiber optics telecommunications system, a computing system.

[34] Annual Report 1977-78 and Five Year Review from the President of [Harrison] University, p. 2. "As of the spring of 1982, 191 sections of 158 undergraduate courses, and 111 sections of 99 graduate courses are offered ..." "Collection Development Policy Statement, [Jackson] Library," March 1982. (Typewritten), p. 2.

[35] Report of the President 1978-79 [Harrison] University, p. 15.

[36] "A partial plan which provided a policy base for the [Fillmore] Campus as a market-oriented extension center was approved by the Council." Self Study 1977, p. 6-3.

University I (Harrison University)   85

[37] Report of the President 1971-1972, The Impact of Austerity, [Harrison] University, p. 17.

[38] Annual Report of the President of [Harrison] University 1976-1977, p. 11.

[39] It is true, as the dean of the Fillmore campus stated, that the Fillmore campus is at a very awkward distance--only some fifteen miles from the Wilson campus--from an architypal urban university to the epitome of suburban America--the same university. Interview with the dean of the Fillmore campus, January 6, 1986.

[40] _____, Assistant Librarian, A Brief History of the Library of [Harrison] University, ([City], 1934), pp. 1-2.

[41] "Outstanding Dates in the History of [Harrison] University and Its Library," March 3, 1981. (Typewritten), p. 4.

[42] "OMS Report," (Office of Management Studies of the Association of Research Libraries), 1980. (Typewritten), p. 6.

[43] The "Office of Management Studies Public Service Study" made the recommendation that the two departments be merged under one department head: "This would allow for one administrative entity for all main campus science libraries .... This does not imply any physical merger." "Office of Management Studies Public Service Study, Conducted by [Harrison] Universities Libraries, Final Report of the Study Team," September 1984. (Typewritten), p. 5.

[44] Quoted in "[Harrison] University Report of the Director of Libraries for 1977/78 and the Decade Since 1968." (Typewritten), p. 15.

⁴⁵ This is due to change very soon, with the reporting of the health sciences center libraries to be to the newly created position of vice-president of health sciences and the dean of the medical school, as the libraries reported some ten years ago.

⁴⁶ The total volume count of the libraries in 1984-85 was 92,341. "Health Sciences Center Library Annual Statistical Report, 1984-1985." (Typewritten), p. 3. In the provost's Proposed Academic Plan, it is planned that the health sciences libraries be consolidated into a single library. Proposed Academic Plan, p. 16.

⁴⁷ Interview with the law librarian, November 14, 1985.

⁴⁸ "Miscellany #2--July 5, 1985; To: All Library Staff; From _____, Director of Libraries." (Typewritten), p. 1. This implements a recommendation in a 1976 report by a consultant that "the Library remain relatively small, depending on referrals to and loans from other [Harrison] collections and the many excellent libraries in the [city] area." Quoted in "Collection Development Policy Statement, [Jackson] Library," March, 1982. (Typewritten), p. 2.

⁴⁹ "Report of _____, Acting Director of Libraries from September, 1976 to May, 1977." (Typewritten), p. 11.

⁵⁰ As stated in the introduction: "The Task Force on Reorganization was charged to undertake a self-examination of the Central Library System ... in January 1980 ... to look at the current organizational structure ..." "OMS Report," p. 1.

⁵¹ The department heads took the initiative and made such a proposal for an interim organization. In a letter to the provost, they

University I (Harrison University)   87

stated: "The Library staff has had to absorb
so many internal changes during the past four
years ... that we believe a demonstration of
continuity is essential to the health of the
organization and, therefore, to the services
it offers. As the group which has functioned
as the Director's cabinet for the past three
years, we believe we have a responsibility to
provide this continuity." (Letter) "To:
_____, Provost of the University; From:
Administrative Council, [Harrison] University
Central Library System," May 24, 1985.
(Typewritten), p. 1.

[52] The management team deferred financial and
some policy decisions as they did not feel
they were vested with the authority to make
major planning policy. Interview with the
head of cataloging, October 31, 1985.

[53] Prior to 1968 the librarian reported to
the president; since 1968 the reporting has
been to the provost or, as that position has
changed title, vice-president of academic
affairs.

[54] Seating the director of libraries on the
council of deans was initiated in 1979 with
the appointment of the new director. Annual
reports of the previous director of libraries
indicate his dissatisfaction with the lack of
communication and information due to the director's exclusion from such councils. "The
library operation has virtually no contact
with academic policy councils, yet the Library is a chief instrument of the academic
program .... the Library operates virtually
in a vacuum except for necessary contacts regarding personnel, fiscal, and physical plant
matters ...." "[Harrison] University, Report
of the Director of Libraries 1975-1976; Confidential Appendix to Accompany the Annual
Report of the Director of Libraries for
1974/75." (Typewritten), p. 1.

[55] Interview with the assistant to the director of libraries, November 21, 1985.

[56] Interview with the director of libraries, October 18, 1985.

[57] Although not for the law, medical, and dental libraries.

[58] However, the budget is established at the Wilson library by the director of libraries.

[59] Interview with the chief of the Fillmore campus library, January 6, 1986.

[60] "Office of Management Studies Public Service Study," p. iii: "... this study has given the Central Library System (CLS) an opportunity to examine itself and to plan for its future within the context of rapidly evolving technologies, new information sources, declining financial resources and changing user needs."

[61] The four task forces were concerned with the organization of public services, staffing and management, public service and technology, and library users and their changing needs. Ibid., pp. iii-iv.

[62] Interview with the director of libraries, October 18, 1985.

[63] Interview with the head of access services, November 14, 1985.

[64] Interview with the head of access services, November 26, 1985.

[65] Ibid.

[66] Interview with the director of libraries, October 18, 1985.

University I (Harrison University) 89

[67] Interview with the acting head of collection development, October 18, 1985.

[68] "[Harrison] University Inter-Office Communication," [From Director of Libraries on a Collection Development Policy], September 25, 1979. (Typewritten), p. 1.

[69] "Book Selection Policy, Technology Library," March 1981; "Collection Development Policy Statement, [Jackson] Library," March 1982; "Film Selection Policy, [Wilson Campus] Film Library," January 16, 1981; "Record Selection Policy, [Wilson Campus] Library Audio Unit," August 1980; "Collection Development Policy Statement, [Fillmore] Campus Library," September 1980. (all Typewritten).

[70] Interview with the director of libraries, October 18, 1985.

[71] "Library Planning // August, 1985," 1985/86. (Typewritten).

[72] Proposed Academic Plan, p. 14.

[73] Ibid., p. 15.

[74] Ibid., p. 52.

[75] A committee on conferences and travel of the Academic Assembly forwarded to the director recommendations to be incorporated into library policy and procedure. "Academic Assembly of Librarians Meeting," September 10, 1985. (Typewritten), p. 2.

[76] Interview with the personnel officer, October 18, 1985. In earlier years of presidential annual reports when the dollar percentage of library support was given, it ranged from 2.2% to 2.3%.

[77] "1985-86 Line Item Budget, Form B-1." (Typewritten), p. 11.

[78] Interview with the director of libraries, December 11, 1985.

[79] Interview with the director of libraries, October 18, 1985.

[80] Interview with the assistant to the director of libraries, November 21, 1985.

[81] The director of libraries in 1980 arranged for all the university libraries to join at the same time. This included the law library and the medical library.

[82] [Harrison] University School of Business Administration, The Ph.D. Program in Business Adminstration, p. 8.

[83] In the 1977/78 Annual Report, the director of libraries wrote: "[The University] joined the Center for Research Libraries nine years ago. The considerable cost (about $12,000 annually) is not justified by the number of loans but is a bargain from the aspect of availability of research materials, which, lacking membership, [the University] would have to buy." "[Harrison] University Report of the Director of Libraries for 1977/78 and the Decade Since 1968." (Typewritten), p. 3.

[84] "Collection Development Policy Statement," [Jackson] Library," March 1982. (Typewritten), p. 3.

[85] "Annual Report 1984-1985, Access Services Department," September 9, 1985. (Typewritten), p. 5. The report anticipates that the introduction of the online system at all libraries "should precipitate a monumental increase in intralibrary loan activity." Ibid.

[86] "Administrative Council Minutes," Tuesday, August 20, 1985. (Typewritten), p. 1. In the Proposed Academic Plan the provost's recommendations include: "Complete the conver-

University I (Harrison University) 91

sion of the card catalogue system to an on-line system, integrating the current serial acquisition system into this facility, and putting serial control capability on-line," p. 15. A $4,000,000 item for equipment to automate [the university] library was the second item included in the provost's lists of equipment needs. Ibid., p. 51.

[87] Proposed Academic Plan, p. 15.

[88] "Recommendations for Extension of Geac to Remote Sites and Collections in [the Library System]," May 20, 1985. (A total of 22 sites when completed.) (Typewritten).

[89] Walk 100 Years in a Hundred Feet, p. 4.

[90] Interview with the chief of the Fillmore campus library, January 6, 1986.

[91] Ibid.

CHAPTER III

INSTITUTION II (CLEMENS UNIVERSITY)

A. THE ENVIRONMENT: THE UNIVERSITY AND ITS SETTING

Background and Description

Clemens University is a private, nonsectarian, coeducational university, with six campuses widely dispersed in urban, suburban, and rural settings, all within five counties in one state in the Northeast (see figure 5). Three are campuses with resident facilities; three are satellite or branch campuses with curriculum and faculty fed by the major campuses.[1] The university owns the properties of the three major campuses, but currently has a rental arrangement for the other three. All campuses operate under one charter; they have one board of trustees and one chief executive officer, the president. The university offers more than 240 undergraduate and graduate programs on all campuses through the masters level in arts and sciences; education; communications, computer and information science; health professions; pharmacy and health sciences; public administration and accountancy; business administration; and visual and performing arts. A Ph.D. program is offered in clinical psychology.

Clemens University, currently with a total enrollment of approximately 20,000 students and more than 1,000 faculty, was founded in a large metropolitan city in 1926

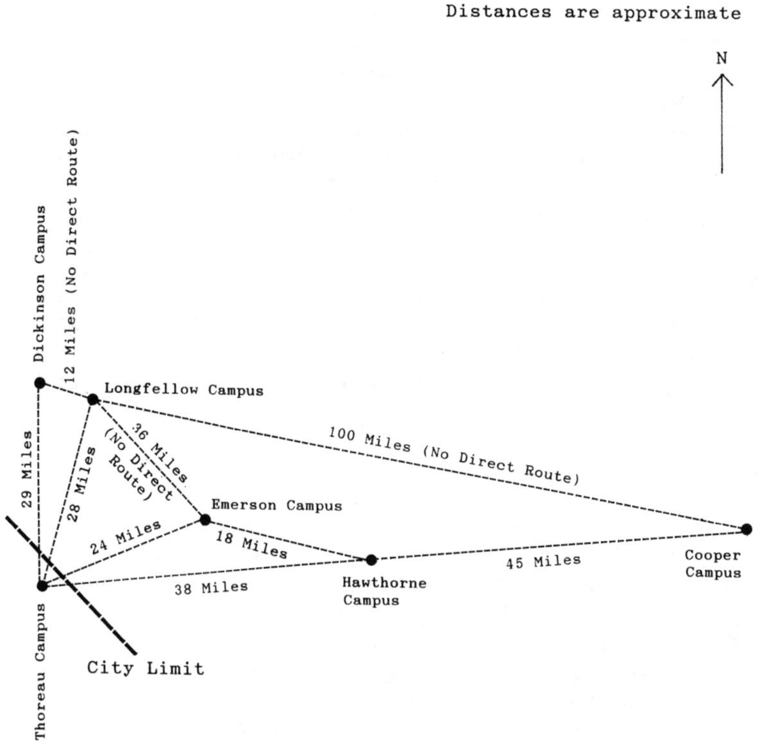

Institution II (Clemens University)

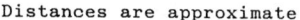

Figure 5
CLEMENS UNIVERSITY
DISTANCES BETWEEN CAMPUSES BY AUTO ROUTE

by a group of civic leaders with the goal of
providing to the community "effective and
modestly priced higher education."[2] This was
the culmination of fifteen years of serious,
determined discussions by a citizens committee. In 1929, a college of pharmacy which
had been established in 1886 became part of
the university, retaining its own board of
trustees and its fiscal autonomy; in 1979 it
relocated to a new complex on the Thoreau
campus and legally merged with the university.

The university grew, surviving the difficult depression years and a calamitous drop
of enrollment during World War II which
forced it into a brief receivership. At the
end of the war the influx of returning ser-
vicemen accelerated the university's return
to financial solvency, enabling it to plan
and implement growth.

The expansion to a multicampus institution occurred in 1954 with the opening of the
Emerson campus twenty-four miles away, followed in 1963 by the establishment of the
Cooper campus over eighty miles distant in an
area of thriving farms and vacation homes.
All three campuses offer undergraduate and
graduate programs to resident and commuter
students. Three additional campuses were
established to serve commuting upper-division
and graduate students: Hawthorne (1972),
Longfellow (1975), and Dickinson (1980). All
of the administrative offices of the university are located at a university center on a
fifteen acre tract acquired in 1966 approximately one-half mile west of the Emerson campus, geographically central to the campuses
yet not attached to any one.

During its history, the university has
undergone restructuring resulting in varying
degrees of centralization and decentralization. In the 1960s in an early attempt to

Institution II (Clemens University)   95

strive for unification throughout the entire
university, additional administrators were
appointed: a vice-chancellor for academic affairs, a vice-chancellor for development,
university graduate deans, and university
directors of public relations and research
administration. In the late 1960s, at the
recommendation of consultants, arrangements
were made to sell the Thoreau urban campus to
a city university since a planned open admissions policy of that public university was
expected to result in severely declining enrollment for the private university. For political and emotional reasons the sale was
not consummated. Some faculty and administrators would have preferred to gain the
financial benefits which would have resulted
had the original urban campus been sold and
the proceeds used to develop the other campuses.

In 1968, consultants presented an organization plan designed to create a stronger
centralized administration. However, instead
of strengthening the central administration,
the board of trustees elected to create a
federalist system and strengthen each campus
by creating the position of president as senior administrator for each of the three major
campuses and the position of chancellor as
the chief executive of the entire university.
In 1969, the then chancellor recommended to
the board of trustees that the university be
dissolved and the three campuses become independent colleges or universities. This was
rejected by the board and the original federalist system with three campus presidents and
one university chancellor retained.

In a 1982 Thoreau Self-Study prepared
for the visiting team of the Middle States
Association,[3] an explanation was given of the
"federalist" organizational structure of the
previous decade identifying those powers and
responsibilities which existed at the campus

level and those under the authority of the university's central administration. A campus was responsible for developing and implementing its academic programs and for developing its annual budgets. The university's central administration, among other obligations, was responsible for bargaining collectively with each of the faculty unions at the individual campuses and for exercising final fiscal authority. It is generally recognized that the campuses were psychologically as well as geographically remote from each other; they perceived themselves as separate independent institutions, with the university's central administration as little more than a holding corporation. As units in a federated structure, the campuses made their own decisions, resulting in different policies formulated in different places. There existed no mechanism for university-wide allocation of resources or assessment of the system as a whole.

A critical 1982 Middle States accreditation report provided the impetus for the complete reorganization of the institution.[4] In 1985 the university submitted to the state's commissioner for higher and professional education an institutional master plan proposing a complete reversal from the previous federated system in which campuses were autonomous to a strong, unified organization.[5] A major problem would be to overcome the provincialism of a faculty who identified only with their own campuses. This was to be accomplished by the creation of university faculties which cut across all campuses under the authority and responsibility of five university deans as chief academic and administrative officers for the faculties: business, public administration and accountancy; education; communications, computer and information sciences; health professions; visual and performing arts. The two major individual campuses, however, would retain a school of

Institution II (Clemens University)   97

arts and sciences with their own faculties. (The library system was not included in the reorganization plan.) The intention was to enable faculty and programs to cross over all the campuses, something that was previously impossible. With cross over, as for instance one university faculty offering computer science programs on the Thoreau campus and on the Emerson campus, the university could provide new depth and breadth of faculty at all campuses. A projected accompanying benefit would be an increasing identification by faculty with the university. Upon approval of the plan by the state commissioner for higher and professional education, the charter of the university was entirely restated and amended in September 1984, "in order to recognize the current form of the University as a system with the flexibility to offer programs in all of the regions served by the six current campuses."[6] In addition, though unrelated to faculty cross over, students would now be permitted to register for a course on any of the campuses of the university.

Student populations of the Thoreau and Emerson campuses are quite different though both campuses serve foreign students from many countries. The Thoreau campus has always been committed to educating the low income student who could not afford to go elsewhere, while the Emerson campus has always attracted the higher income student who could not academically qualify for an ivy-league school.

The composition of the undergraduate student body of the Thoreau campus has been described as: "Over 50% ... come from families with annual incomes below $12,000; a substantial number are from homes where the annual income is less than $9,000."[7] The campus historically has had a working class population from its local area, with a high percentage of minority and Asian students.[8] The ethnic composition has changed as the ethnic composition of the city's public school system has changed.

The Emerson campus, in addition to a predominantly middle class student body, has always had a large part-time adult population. Its early programs were directed toward that constituency with a week-end college program. Cooper campus also has a traditional middle class college population, although this may change as a result of its recruitment among different population and age groups. Common to all the major campuses is a large number of first-generation college students who are the only members of their family to pursue studies at the college level.[9] The satellite non-resident campuses were developed principally to provide upper-division and graduate programs to commuting and working part-time students, a large component of the student bodies of the other campuses as well.

Organization and Administration of the University

The restructuring that resulted in 1984 was master-minded by the then chairman of the board of trustees. He created an organizational framework that was similar to a corporate organization: a chief executive officer who is the president of the university (replacing the position of chancellor), and two chief operating officers who govern the two major geographic divisions of that university (see figure 6). Two major campuses (Thoreau and Emerson) were each given responsibility for two smaller campuses, dividing the university into an eastern region (Emerson, Cooper, and Hawthorne) and a western region (Thoreau, Longfellow, and Dickinson). The two senior administrators on the two major campuses who previously had the title of

Institution II (Clemens University) 99

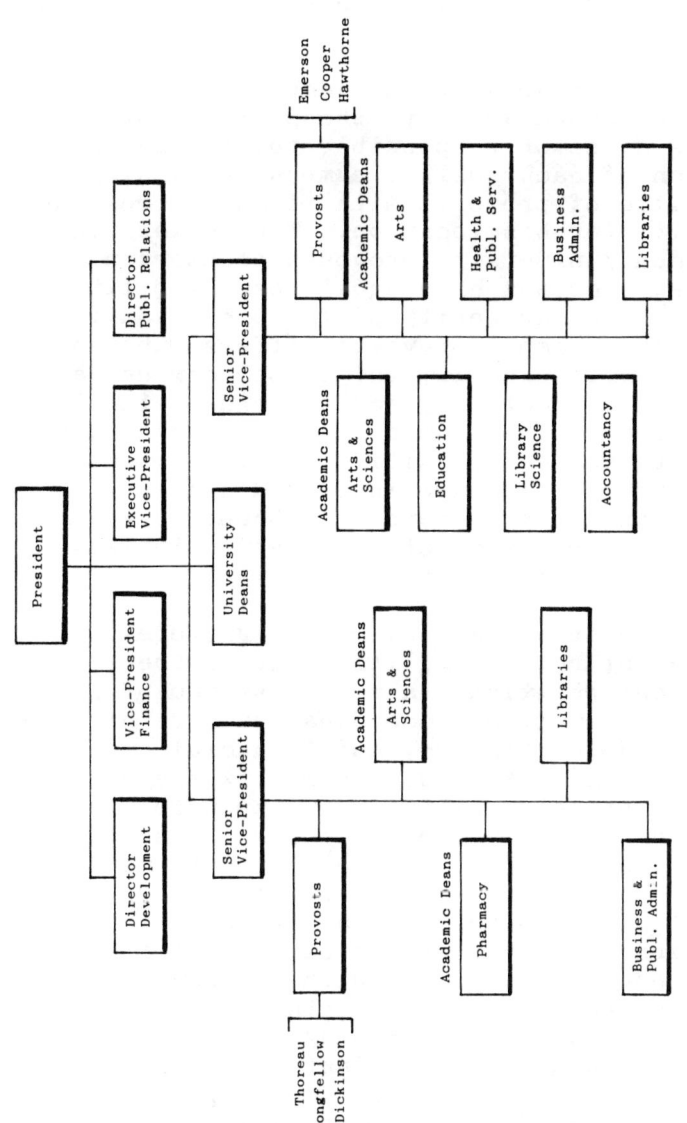

Figure 6
ORGANIZATION CHART: CLEMENS UNIVERSITY

president were now designated senior vice-president/university provost, one for the eastern region and the other for the western region.

To provide a greater degree of administrative accountability, the position of the campus director responsible for the administration of each smaller campus was assigned the title of provost, with financial responsibility for his location. The senior vice-president/university provosts of Emerson and Thoreau campuses have equal responsibilities; the scope of authority of the other individual branch campus provosts differs substantially. For example, the Cooper campus has a resident student body and a resident faculty, whereas the other three branch campuses have neither resident faculties nor a resident student body, and are in rented quarters. Consequently, the provost at Cooper has a much broader jurisdictional responsibility than the other provosts.

This organization, by design, creates overlap of responsibilities within the different positions--a matrix system of horizontal and vertical coordination for the academic, administrative, and financial operations.[10] The effect of the matrix system is that no one person has sole responsibility nor are there clear unambiguous lines of command. For example, the position of university dean with responsibility for faculties at all six campuses overlays with the campus provosts where both their responsibilities intersect.[11] Deans meet with the senior vice-president/university provosts of the east or west to negotiate their budgets. Even though they report to the president of the university (until the position of vice-president for academic affairs is created), they are supervised by the east and west senior vice-president/university provosts in respect to the daily operation, the budget, and the fac-

Institution II (Clemens University)

ulty they hire. In the planning of the reorganization, it was decided that there would be no vice-president of academic affairs to diffuse authority among the different faculties. It appears that this will not be a permanent arrangement, as the lack of that academic position results in reporting congestion at the top with all deans and all provosts reporting to the president.[12]

Before the reorganization of the previous federated system, the campuses operated autonomously without centralization or direct control. They were held together in an administrative sense only through the central office and the budget planning process, and by being a component of a single corporation with one board of trustees. Under the new system, the base of instructional operations remains at the campus level, but policy and promulgation of policy is now created and carried out by the university officers in close liaison with the university deans and the provosts of the campuses.

Under the university's previous structure, it was not possible to move personnel, materials, or budgetary resources from one campus to another, nor was it possible for a student registered at one campus to take courses at another. It is the intent of the new system to overcome those limitations, while recognizing the geographic distribution of the campuses. One limitation remains--the existence of a separate faculty union on each of the three major campuses. A letter from the previous chancellor of the university to the president of the Thoreau campus faculty federation expressed the administration's conviction that a single collective bargaining agent and contract would result in a stronger university.[13] Separate faculty unions, however, are still in existence.

Clemens University is an example of a consolidated system, although to some the Emerson campus is viewed as the most important campus of the university since that is where the financial strength and the prestige of the university are centered. In addition, the administration offices are located on the edge of that campus at university center. The eastern region under the leadership of the Emerson campus generates about two-thirds of the university's enrollment revenue, and thus wields a weightier influence budgetarily than the western region. Consequently, over the past decade the Emerson campus has been the dominant campus in the sense that it has been generating the revenues that sustain the university, while two other campuses, Cooper and Thoreau, have been operating at deficits.

For many years each campus was known by a name that deliberately was not identified with the university's name, an overt form of dissociation. A vital component of the reorganization plan was the attempt by the board of trustees to give the name of the university the major identity, not the name of the campus.[14] This issue was treated in the "Report to [Clemens] University" by the Middle States Team in a section "Identity Crisis," in which they observed:

> ... loyalties to the individual educational Centers supersede any loyalty to [Clemens] University as a whole. Further, in one Center, at least, loyalty to the schools within that Center seems to overshadow the Center as a whole, let alone any feelings about the University.[15]

With the recent reorganization, the university's ninth president took office on July 1, 1985. The previous president, in his financial report to the board of trustees, re-

Institution II (Clemens University)   103

viewed the changes that had occurred in the university's organization:

> ... the University emerge[d] from its disarray under the national impulse to centrifugal autonomies in 1969-71, then through a decade of successful operation as a federation of campuses and, in 1983-84, well into reorganization as a single University with Faculties ...[16]

Elements of political tension have existed among the campuses from the beginning of the multicampus configuration. In particular, rivalry and a psychological division between the Thoreau campus and the Emerson campus have long been present. The university consisted in the beginning of only the Thoreau campus; then that campus started branch campuses, the first in 1954 with the Emerson campus. That the new branch campus was built by the president of the Thoreau campus and by the faculty of that campus is remembered with some rancor by some administrators of the Thoreau campus and in the university center, for when the Thoreau campus had experienced substantial surpluses, it established the Emerson campus and continued financial and logistical support; yet when the Thoreau campus fell upon hard times, the Emerson campus, considering the Thoreau campus a perennial drain of resources was reluctant to come to the assistance of Thoreau campus.[17]

The Emerson campus has been able to generate an annual surplus which has contributed considerably to reducing the university's cumulative deficit;[18] that these surpluses are not returned directly to the Emerson campus is a source of irritation to that campus. The 1982 Self-Study commented upon a multicampus phenomenon:

> ... there is a concern involving the overall financial structure of [Clemens] University .... Although [Emerson campus] appears to be financially solvent, the other two Centers might possibly not fare as well in the future and, therefore, under these circumstances the responsibilities of one Center to the entire University is a matter of grave concern to [Emerson campus].[19]

The recent creation of university deans and university faculties is expected to ease the tension between the two campuses.

Clemens University is approximately 85% tuition-dependent, with insignificant resources in endowments. The administration realizes that for an institution with a budget over $100 million a year, their endowments are small indeed.[20] To counter this lag in endowments, the new president is placing emphasis upon fund raising, and has appointed a new vice-president of external affairs and a supporting development staff. In this way he is attempting to avoid financial problems similar to those in 1982-83 when the university was faced with a $7 million deficit. (Through large scale elimination of positions, reduction of operating costs and by improving revenues, that deficit was limited to under $1 million.)[21] The younger branch campuses are considered the growth areas. To offset university budget deficits, new programs were started at sites which became identified as [Clemens] University at [name of] campus; the university is proud of its record of prodigious development of new programs which are creative and innovative.[22]

The university receives a considerable amount of federal and state aid,[23] including monies from the Tuition Assistance Program (TAP) directly to students, and state aid to students (approximately 5% of the university

Institution II (Clemens University)   105

budget) in the form of capitation grants.[24]
As over 50% of the enrollment at the Thoreau
campus consists of minority students, that
campus actively seeks grants designed to support them. The United States Department of
Education has designated the campus a "Developing Institution," and the campus has received several substantial grants under the
provisions of Title III of the Higher Education Act of 1976 which was originally instituted to assist black schools in the south.

   Equal opportunity does not exist for all
member campuses to secure resources from the
system's central administration as two of the
major campuses have been operating in the red
while the third campus enjoys a surplus. It
appears that the Emerson campus, with the
greatest number of students, and therefore
the income-producing campus, has been receiving the greatest share of funds. University
resources have not been shared across the
board, each campus receiving funding that was
appropriate to its financial contribution
rather than to its needs. (This has been
particularly apparent in the support of the
campus libraries, as will be observed in the
library summary.) The university is cognizant that the Emerson campus is the safeguard of the economy and well-being of the
entire operation, and treats it accordingly.

Description of the Campuses

Thoreau Campus

   Thoreau campus, the original unit of the
multicampus university, is the only urban
campus of Clemens University, with the majority of its students from the surrounding
metropolitan area (4,500 undergraduate and
2,000 graduate students). Its campus occupies a twenty-two acre site in a badly dete-

riorated area of the city. Buildings on the campus, in addition to a learning center which houses the library, consist of several eleven-story classroom centers, two smaller structures, and a newer nine-story arts and humanities building. Degrees offered include associate and bachelor of arts, bachelor of science, master of arts, master of science, master of science in education, and doctor of philosophy (in clinical psychology), associate in applied science, bachelor of science in business and in computer science, master of business administration, master of science in accounting and in taxation, and master of public administration. The college of pharmacy and health sciences offers degrees in pharmaceutics, pharmacy administration, physical education, physical therapy, biomedical communications, community health, and pharmaceutical administration or hospital pharmacy administration.

The university's problems of contraction are due to a great extent to the Thoreau campus. At one point in the post World War II period that campus had an enrollment of almost 10,000 students; in the early 1970s, as a result of open enrollment in the competing city university, it dropped to 4,000 students. The enrollment is still low and the Thoreau campus still operates under a deficit budget.

To assist disadvantaged students the Thoreau campus has developed special programs in admissions and financial aid and provides extensive support services. New programs in the sciences have been instituted, largely supported by grants; major grants have included a Minority Access to Research Careers, funded by the National Institute of Health, and Title III funded programs in molecular biology and in computer science.

Institution II (Clemens University)

Emerson Campus

The Emerson campus, on over 400 acres, was established on a country estate purchased a few years after Clemens University began offering extension programs in that area to meet the needs of veterans of World War II. After extensive litigation with residents who objected to the establishment of a university in their residential neighborhood, the first class in September 1954 was formed with 121 day students and 98 evening students, eight full-time faculty (this included the dean, librarian and registrar), and six part-time faculty. Ten years later, a class of more than one thousand graduated, with new facilities provided for the sciences and engineering, and a library with a capacity of over one million volumes.

The perception of separation of the campuses at University II can be said to date back to the foundation of Emerson campus. From the beginning of the college, the students "never really thought of themselves as being a part of [Clemens] University ..."[25] but rather of the campus only.

The Emerson campus continued to offer evening extension courses in local school systems and opened in 1957 on the grounds of an air force base the first private, degree-granting college physically situated on a military installation in the United States. Plans for a university law center on that site never materialized and the entire operation was terminated in 1964.

More than seventy-five programs leading to the baccalaureate and graduate degrees are offered in education, business and accountancy, arts and sciences, public administration, and library science. Special areas of concentration include computers in education, counseling, criminal justice, management, engineering, public administration/health care administration, special education, and taxation.

In the 1982 "Report of the Middle States Association Evaluation Team Visit" to the Emerson campus, before the restructuring of the university occurred, the team observed that it was a unique campus, dependent upon the university for its Middle States Association accreditation, while its programs were registered with the state department of education separate from the other components of the university, and having a distinctly Emerson campus faculty with their own collective bargaining contract.[26]

Cooper Campus

Located on 110 acres near the ocean in a seaside resort over an hour's drive from the Emerson campus, the Cooper campus was founded in 1963 to offer undergraduate programs in marine and environmental sciences and in the fine arts. Two years earlier a group of residents had formed an organization to obtain a college of liberal arts in their area. Their arrangements with the university provided funds for a suitable campus site and an estate was acquired for the campus. The college opened in September 1963 with 313 students and twelve full-time faculty. Today it additionally offers graduate programs in education and business administration and has an undergraduate and graduate student body of 1200, a high percentage of whom are resident students.

Several construction projects are in the planning stage, namely expanding the marine science station and providing new classroom and laboratory space and a new fine arts building. This will be the first new building in a decade of serious financial and enrollment problems for the campus. In 1983

Institution II (Clemens University)

when the university experienced a $1.3 million revenue shortfall in its $100 million budget, the top administrative officer of the campus (then termed "president") was removed and the university trustees ordered the college to be merged into the Emerson campus. It is now part of the eastern division of the campuses under the administration of the senior vice-president/university provost of the Emerson campus but with its own provost.

The Cooper campus historically has been a marginal money loser. Of the $100 million university budget, approximately $600,000 is the budget deficit for that campus--costs not covered by campus income. However, the new president has expressed his commitment to make that campus succeed; the provost of the campus is encouraged by the president's intention of steadily reinvesting in the campus so that it can attract more students.[27]

In the spring of 1986 the president of the university appointed to the unsalaried position of part-time chancellor of the campus a former United States ambassador whose immediate goal was to increase the enrollment of that campus and to improve its image.[28] This signaled the president's determination to achieve finally the growth for that campus that had been anticipated when it was created twenty years ago.

Hawthorne Campus

The Hawthorne campus is situated on the grounds of a convent approximately a thirty-minute drive from the Emerson campus. In 1959 the university had begun to offer upper-division (junior and senior students) and master's degree programs in the Hawthorne area in high schools. In 1972 the university formed a unique partnership - a "Coordinate Campus" - with a parochial college situated on the grounds of a novitiate in Hawthorne to provide such upper-division and graduate programs for two-year community colleges in the region. In 1977 the university successfully petitioned the state department of education to accredit the Hawthorne facility as one of the university's multicampuses, the Hawthorne campus. The parochial college has since moved, and only the university campus remains, using the space previously occupied by both institutions. Its facilities are housed on several floors within one building at the end of the convent complex, with additional space available from the convent when needed.

The student body numbers approximately 1,200, about 250 of whom are full-time undergraduates and 200 part-time undergraduates, and approximately 700 graduate students, most of whom are part-time. The undergraduate students predominantly are graduates of local two-year community colleges. Bachelor degree programs are offered in accounting and business, criminal justice and political science, with master's degree programs in accounting, taxation, business administration, criminal justice, health care/public administration, and courses in library science and education (bilingual education, special education, reading, school administration, school counseling, elementary education).

Longfellow Campus

As a result of a formal agreement in 1974 between the Thoreau campus of Clemens University and a multicampus college in Longfellow county which offers undergraduate programs only, the university provides master's degree and graduate certificate programs at the main campus of that college. The agreement governs the use of space, registration and bursarial services, use of the library, and the personnel to support the courses offered. Any surplus or deficit remaining after payment of direct expenses is

Institution II (Clemens University)

apportioned equally between the college and the university. The immediate success of the programs led in 1979 to the state board of regents designating the site as a branch campus of the Thoreau campus. The campus has its own provost appointed by Clemens University with responsibility for that campus. The Longfellow campus remains in the western region under the aegis of the senior vice-president/university provost of the Thoreau campus.

With an enrollment of approximately 1,000 students, graduate programs are offered in business and public administration, biology, chemistry, bilingual and special education, counseling, health professions, psychology, criminal justice, pharmacy, and library science.

Dickinson Campus

The Dickinson campus, located approximately an hour's drive from the Emerson campus and in another county, offers graduate programs only, with courses leading to master's degrees in business administration, public administration, health care administration, library and information science, elementary education, school administration, special education, and professional accountancy.

The newest of the university's six campuses, it was started in 1980 as an extension of the Emerson campus on the grounds of a parochial college a mile away from its present location. Currently housed on two floors of a renovated excessed parochial high school building, it has more than 500 students, almost all part-time, enrolled in graduate programs, with completion of degree requirements for certain programs stipulating course attendance at some of the university's other campuses. Although since 1974 the larger Emerson campus has offered graduate courses in this county to part-time students who are, for the most part, full-time working professionals, the Dickinson campus was not granted branch status until 1981. As a result of the university's reorganization, the campus is now under the jurisdiction of the western division of the university, reporting to the senior vice-president/university provost of the Thoreau campus.

B. THE UNIVERSITY LIBRARIES: STRUCTURES AND PROCESSES

Clemens University's libraries evolved from a single library at the original campus (Thoreau) shortly after the first classes were offered in 1927. For one year the university occupied one floor of a city-owned building. When the university moved into its own building in 1928, the library occupied half of the administrative floor. The original small collection was acquired through gifts; acquisitions increased the size until in 1941 the library's collection had grown to more than 16,000 volumes.

As a result of a decrease in student enrollment during World War II, the university was forced into receivership. The building was sold and the university moved into rented quarters. All of its physical possessions, including about 90% of the library's 17,000 books, were placed in storage. The remainder was placed in faculty offices and in a small room assigned for essential library reference.

At the end of the war, with increased income through renewed enrollment, the university was able to resume its growth. The books were taken out of storage. Unfortunately, only approximately 10,000 were available when the library was reorganized on the

Institution II (Clemens University)

tenth floor of the next university building; the rest had been damaged beyond use.

A succession of moves into larger quarters followed as the university expanded, until the library was housed in four floors of a building, with holdings divided among rooms on the first, eighth, tenth, and eleventh floors. With a total of 60,000 volumes by the 1960s it became necessary to erect a library building. After many interruptions and political machinations over a period of years, the construction of the current building was completed in 1975. In the meantime the university had expanded into a multicampus institution with multicampus libraries.

Description of the Campus Libraries

Thoreau Campus Library

The Thoreau campus library is located today in a five-story building, the top three floors constituting the library. The building, completed in 1975, is one of the newest on campus, providing 1,000 user spaces and shelving for 450,000 volumes. It houses, in addition to the library, classrooms, tutoring and computer centers, media auditoriums, and studios for photography, graphics, television and audio production. Because of the combination of all these facilities, it has been named the Library Learning Center.

The library has a collection of over 340,000 volumes, microfilms, recordings, films, videotapes, reproductions, and government and United Nations document collections, with library resources directed primarily toward the subject areas of pharmacy and allied health sciences, business, psychology, and education. While special research collections are not actively sought, the holdings do include several special collections that support programs in urban studies, communications, public administration, music, and pharmacy. In addition, as the original library for the university, it has had the opportunity to build collections in history and literature.

The number of staff of the Thoreau library (see figure 7) has declined from sixteen professional and eleven clerical positions in 1981 to nine professional and six clerical positions in 1985, a situation of concern to the outgoing library chief,[29] and one that reflects the strained financial condition of the campus during the past five years. The loss in the number of staff positions coupled with the reduction in budget has resulted in the library currently requiring much attention in terms of collection, organization, and administration.

In 1985 the Thoreau campus library and the library of an art, architecture, and engineering institute located nearby, at the urging of the presidents of the two institutions, explored the potential benefits of integrating their libraries, with particular emphasis upon sharing automation and collection development. After considerable discussions, such a merger was not deemed feasible by either party.[30]

When budget constraints mandated a decrease in the number of hours the library would be open, a grant from a nearby medical school enabled the library to operate additional hours; reciprocally, special collections of materials were prepared for the medical students' use in a lounge area set aside for their quiet study. The issue of increased financial support of the library by the campus and university remains a current problem.

Institution II (Clemens University) 115

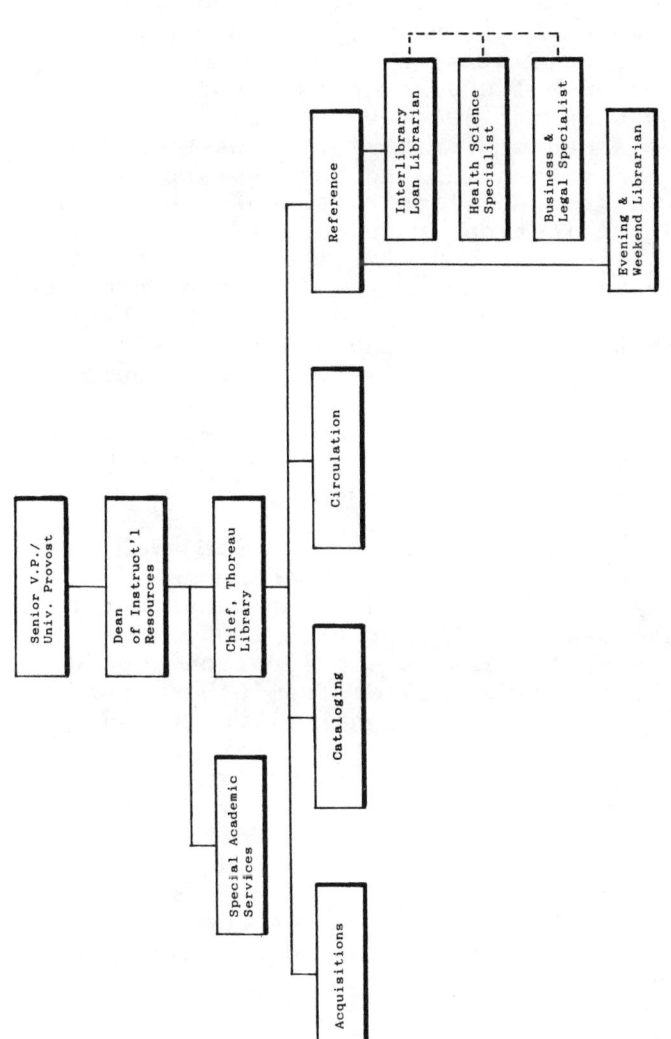

Figure 7
ORGANIZATION CHART: CLEMENS UNIVERSITY, THOREAU CAMPUS LIBRARY

Emerson Campus Library

The Emerson campus Georgian style library is one of the largest and most imposing buildings on that campus, with a capacity of one-and-a-half million volumes and accommodation for over 1,000 students. Special features within its 600,000 volume collection include a center for business research library, an accounting and tax research library, a graduate library school library, a special collections room, and an instructional materials center. The center for business research library resulted from a merger in 1978 of a former county research library of some 250,000 books and documents with the Emerson campus library's business resources. The government documents depository collection is extensive since the library selects 75-80% of the categories offered. Periodical subscriptions number almost 5,000.

The original library with its small book collection was housed in three rooms of a building that had been a guest house for the original owner of the property. For the first several years, the collection depended upon gifts and duplicates from other libraries. From one professional librarian who also taught English for the first three years, the library staff (see figure 8) has grown to seventy-five full-time members (thirty-one professionals and forty-four support staff). On the whole, the Emerson campus library has enjoyed good financial support despite several budget cuts in recent years when the campus experienced enrollment shortfalls.

The Emerson campus library began in 1980 to develop an online circulation and catalog system for its use. At the present time, only the Hawthorne, Dickinson, and Cooper campuses have access to the system via terminals.

Institution II (Clemens University)

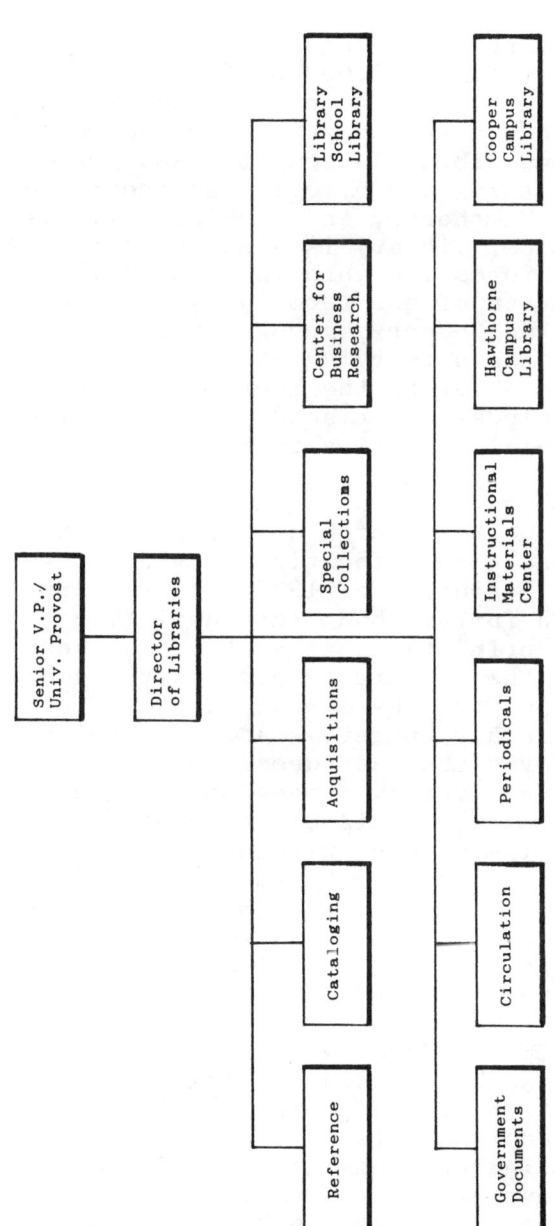

Figure 8
ORGANIZATION CHART: CLEMENS UNIVERSITY, EMERSON CAMPUS LIBRARY

Cooper Campus Library

The library has a collection of more than 135,000 volumes, 1,000 periodicals, serials, newspapers, and government documents. In 1985 its new computer was connected to the Emerson campus library's computer and now can access the catalog and circulation records of the Emerson, Hawthorne, and Dickinson libraries. The Cooper library is also entering its cataloging information into the database. The installation of the terminal will eventually permit the Cooper campus library to become part of the network which was established by the chief of the Emerson campus library and includes other academic, governmental, and special libraries in the region.

To compensate for a decade of inadequate financial support for book collections, an additional one-time allocation of $35,000 was given at the beginning of 1985 to the Cooper library, with further budgetary assistance anticipated during the next years. The new president of the university has visited not only the campus but the library as well to talk about library budget, staff, and building needs. Over the past decade proposals for much needed library expansion have been discussed; the two levels of the present building are inadequate, with nearly 10% of the collection stored in basements of other buildings across the campus. Now plans have been given top priority again to provide an addition to the library or build a new facility, as had been planned in 1982.

In addition to problems of budgets and space, staffing has been a concern. The staff consists of three professionals and four nonprofessionals (see figure 9), which creates staffing problems at the reference and public service desks for all the hours the library is open. Although as a member of OCLC (Online Computer Library Center) the li-

Institution II (Clemens University) 119

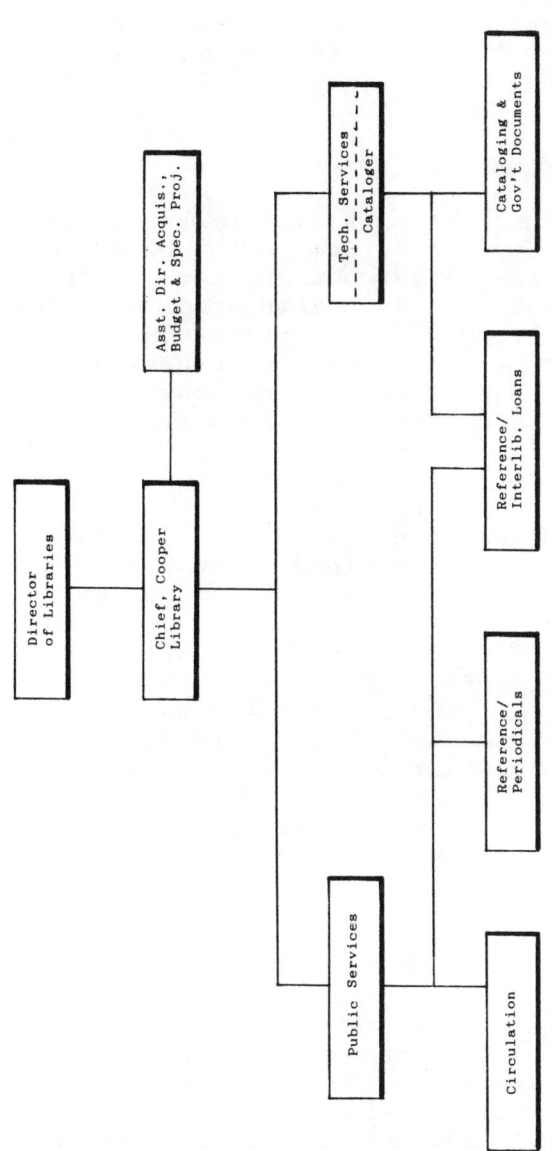

Figure 9
ORGANIZATION CHART: CLEMENS UNIVERSITY, COOPER CAMPUS LIBRARY

brary since 1981 has cataloged its own collection, current discussion is taking place concerning centralized acquisitions, cataloging and processing by the Emerson campus library. Consequently, staffing needs may change.

Hawthorne Campus Library

The Hawthorne campus library has a space problem. Located in a room in the building which houses the classrooms and administrative offices of the campus, the facility provides a small reading area, stack space for a collection of more than 40,000 volumes, and microfilm and microfiche collections of periodicals. It is administered by a professional librarian who reports to the chief of the Emerson campus library and attends all Emerson campus library professional staff meetings. In addition, the Hawthorne staff includes another professional librarian plus one full-time clerk.

Although Hawthorne initiates all book orders, the Emerson campus library provides acquisitions, cataloging and processing for the campus; periodical subscriptions are placed at the Hawthorne campus. The students have access to the Emerson campus library some eighteen miles away, should they elect to go directly there instead of relying upon intercampus loan.

Dickinson Campus Library

Initially, the Dickinson branch campus used the library collection of the parochial college which housed the university's classes. In September 1984 a library collection of nearly 4,000 titles was assembled in the university's new quarters in a building removed from the parochial college, 153 new periodical subscriptions were entered, and approximately 2,000 reels of older titles on

Institution II (Clemens University) 121

microfilm were received from the Emerson campus. Contractual provisions have been made for the students to continue to have access to all services of the library of the parochial college.

The library is connected to the Emerson campus library by computer, and thereby is able to locate materials on that campus. These are subsequently received through courier deliveries several times a week. Although there is no computer connection to the Thoreau campus at this time, Dickinson is able to request periodical articles from a printed list that is available.

As a result of the reorganization plans, the campus was designated a part of the western region with the Thoreau campus as the lead campus. However, services such as acquisitions and cataloging continue to be carried out by the Emerson campus library of the eastern region. The library chief of the Emerson campus informed his library faculty at a meeting that the Dickinson campus library was still under the jurisdiction of the Emerson campus library.[31]

Longfellow Campus Library

The university has made an agreement with the library of a host college in Longfellow county whereby the university provides approximately $40,000 a year to buy materials which become part of the permanent collection of the college.[32] The library director of that college makes the decisions about acquisitions of materials. Students of the university taking courses at that site have full library privileges at the college library. The university does have a provost on the campus who works in coordination with the library director of that college.

Organization, Governance and Administrative Structure of the Libraries

During much of this research, the position of university librarian did not exist, but was created immediately after the new president assumed office in July 1985. Before the appointment of a university librarian, the lines of reporting of each of the campus library chiefs differed. The chief of the Emerson campus library, for example, (who was later appointed to the new position of university director of libraries by the president) reported to the senior vice-president/ university provost of the Emerson campus. The Thoreau campus library chief reported to the dean of instructional resources, who, in turn, reported to the senior vice-president/ university provost of that campus. On that campus it is the dean of instructional resources, instead of the campus library chief, who sits on the senior vice-president/ university provost's administrative council. (The council consists of library, head of computers, academic coordinator, budget officer, admissions officer, and local campus deans.) The fact that the library chief of the Thoreau campus reported to the dean of instructional resources and was not therefore included in the campus college deans and directors' meetings, was perceived by the library chief as an indication of the lack of status accorded the library and a source of personal frustration.[33] At the time of interviewing, the library chief of the Thoreau campus had submitted his resignation, and the library was placed immediately under the direct responsibility of the dean of instructional resources. The dean of instructional resources indicated that he did not intend to fill that vacancy immediately, but planned to run the library for the foreseeable future.[34] If a chief of the Thoreau campus library were to be appointed, the policy of having the librarian report to the dean of instructional

Institution II (Clemens University)

resources would probably change, and he/she would in all likelihood report to the university director of libraries.

Previous library chiefs of the Thoreau campus had reported to the senior vice-president/university provost of the Thoreau campus (or the equivalent position of the chief executive), until the appointment of the most recent library chief (who has now resigned). It was the current senior vice-president/university provost who changed that reporting relationship in order to combine responsibilities for all instructional resources.[35]

During the past five years there has been extensive restructuring of positions and reassigning of people in the Thoreau campus library to compensate for the loss of fourteen positions since September 1981. The staff currently consists of ten professionals, including the position of director, and six clerical staff who are shared with instructional resources. The professional staff comprise acquisitions librarian; cataloger; circulation librarian; head of reference (also designated coordinator of public services with responsibility for the positions of interlibrary loan, health science specialist, business and legal specialist); and evening and weekend librarian.

The library chiefs of two smaller campus libraries had an ambiguous reporting relationship; the chief of the Hawthorne campus library reported to the director of the Emerson campus library; the chief of the Dickinson library was unclear about his line of reporting, since while his campus had recently been placed in the western region, the Emerson campus library in the eastern division was still responsible for his library's technical services. (There is no library chief at the Longfellow campus as that library is run by the host Longfellow county college.)

The organizational structure and internal administration of each campus library is dependent upon the size of its staff. The Emerson campus library is organized in distinct departments (acquisitions, cataloging, reference, circulation, government documents, serials, library school library, center for business research, instructional materials center, special collections) administered by thirty-one full-time professionals and a forty-four full-time clerical staff. As there are no assistant director positions, all department heads report to the chief of the library, as do the library chiefs of Cooper and Hawthorne. This broad span of control has been criticized in a committee report in which a recommendation was made for the appointment of an assistant director of libraries,[36] although no such position has been created.

The Cooper campus library includes, in addition to the chief of the library, three professional librarians and four support staff. The president and the administration are now aware of the need for additional staff for that library and have promised assistance. The Hawthorne campus library has two full-time librarians (including the library chief) and one full-time clerk. The Dickinson campus library is the smallest of all, a one and 1/2 librarian operation. All of the libraries are assigned graduate assistants to perform paraprofessional duties.

The new president expressed his firm intention, even before he had taken office, that the libraries operate within a system. As one of his first decisions upon taking office in July 1985, he appointed the chief of the Emerson campus library as the university director of libraries in order to create that university-wide library system.[37] The mandate under which he had assumed the presidency was

Institution II (Clemens University)

that of bringing the institution together, and it was his opinion that nothing serves as a better symbol of the linkage between the campuses than the library system. At the Emerson campus library, the chief of the library reported to the senior vice-president/ university provost until his appointment on July 29, 1985 to the position of university director of libraries; in the new position he reports to the president of the university, pending the creation of the position of vice-president of academic affairs.

At the time of this research, all lines of authority and reporting within the university libraries were not finalized and clarification of authority awaited the ultimate decisions of the new university director of libraries. Though chief administrative officer of the new library system, he was expected to retain his previous responsibilities for the Emerson campus library. Until the reporting relationships of the branch libraries are clearly specified, there will continue to be ambiguity.

The Dickinson library chief has had very little contact with the director of the Emerson campus library; due to the geographic distance from the other campuses, his primary responsibility, by default, is to his provost. Furthermore, because of the small size of the Dickinson campus, the library chief is also head of the computer center, alumni director, and AV director, thus working even more closely with his provost. To add to the confusion, the budget of the Dickinson campus is currently decided by the senior vice-president/university provost of the Thoreau campus; the budget for the campus library is then determined by the provost of the Dickinson campus.

The chief of the Hawthorne campus library is aware of the need for diplomacy in his relationship with his provost, although he realizes his direct line of reporting is to the chief of the Emerson campus library. Fortunately, the provost of the Hawthorne campus concurs that the primary obligation of the library chief is to the chief of the Emerson campus library and thereby has eliminated a potential problem.[38] At the Cooper campus the chief of the library sits on the campus provost's staff and maintains a strong informational relationship with him concerning library matters. This system of organization with lines crossing, frequently referred to by administrators of the university as a matrix system, applies the university concept that the theory of redundancy will strengthen the organization.

Only at the Emerson campus library does the professional staff participate formally in the planning and program development of the campus library, probably due to the fact that it is the only library staff in the university of any significant size. At monthly meetings of the department heads both departmental and library problems are discussed, with minutes of the meetings circulated afterward. The department heads then convey the sense and resolutions of the meetings to their library faculty during individual departmental meetings which serve also to provide a forum for professional staff participation. This close liaison is augmented by monthly library faculty meetings which all professional librarians attend. The relationship between the library chief and the professional staff in that library is excellent, due in no small part to the accessibility of the library chief. Even though in the Emerson campus library the chief has all decision-making powers, he delegates autonomy to each department in the daily running. As campus library chief he sets goals and objectives; planning and procedures are then developed in the monthly meetings with

Institution II (Clemens University)

department heads and, as exigencies demand, in individual meetings.

At the Thoreau campus library, currently without a chief librarian, administrative policies are being established by the dean of instructional resources. Prior to the departure of the library chief, ad hoc committees for collection development, budget, and acquisitions functioned occasionally. The relationship between the library administration and the professional staff in the Thoreau campus library has been poor due to personnel conflicts, budget deficiencies, and the perception of a general lack of leadership.

The chief of the Cooper campus library holds meetings with his small staff every two weeks during semesters to discuss developments in the campus and library. At the Cooper campus library, decision-making is a cooperative process by the small library staff and a faculty library committee, in conference with the library chief.

Until the university-wide library system is established, the processes and agencies of decision-making that directly affect the libraries function at the campus level, except those for budgets, which are imposed and approved at the university level. As at this time the balance between centralization and local campus authority is undetermined, the degree of autonomy with which each campus library will operate remains in question, awaiting the decisions of the new university director of libraries. Local campus authority and local needs, for the most part, have been the rule in the libraries, with campus libraries controlling their collection development, scheduling, and other administrative matters. A manifestation of that autonomy is their establishment of policies and practices independent of each other. However, as the entire university is gearing up for centralization, the library system has been advised by the new president to begin planning for such centralization.

The relationship between the campus librarians and the campus academic departments varies among the campus libraries. At one time the Emerson campus library appointed representatives to each of the disciplines but this representation has not been maintained due to lack of interest by the academic departments. As the library professional staff are in the faculty union and are on faculty committees, they are able to maintain a collegial relationship. Within departmental libraries--the library science library and the center for business research library--librarians work closely with the faculty of each department and maintain strong relationships. On the Cooper campus the provost includes the library chief in meetings with the academic divisions; with a resident faculty such interaction is more effective. Within the Thoreau campus library, in contrast, there is little contact between librarians and faculty. This may have historical reasons, as a previous library chief created an attitude of no interference and no suggestions.

The extent to which the libraries have been involved in planning on a coordinated and cooperative system-wide basis has been minimal. An exceptional occurrence was the preparation for the most recent Middle States visit when the previous chancellor established a library task force consisting of the library chiefs of the Emerson, Thoreau, and Cooper campuses and three additional members. The charge to this task force stated:

> To explore University wide centralized processing of library resources and to coordinate cooperative resource-sharing and collection development, building

Institution II (Clemens University)   129

> upon our respective strengths. To continue to develop the 'multi-type library network' with [Clemens] University as the host computerized library center.[39]

The committee made proposals for greater library interaction, although little materialized at that time. But only a year later, in 1984, under the impetus of the chief of the Emerson campus library (later to become university director of libraries), the chiefs of the Cooper and the Thoreau campus libraries met with him to discuss automation for the university libraries. They jointly developed grant requests and, for the first time, worked together to plan for future facsimile reproduction and other hardware required to connect the libraries through university-wide automation. After several meetings, a network was formed, but the Thoreau campus library had not continued as a participant at the time of this study due to lack of financial commitment by its campus administration. Through the computer terminal connection of Emerson with Cooper, Hawthorne, and Dickinson, those libraries have become a system, regionally speaking. The campuses in the eastern region (plus Dickinson of the western region) work together as a system more effectively than the campuses in the western region; this is partly due to the more active exercise of control by the chief of the Emerson campus library over its branch campus libraries. However, it is the consensus of all interviewed that the various libraries on all the campuses do not yet constitute a system.

Collection Development

The demand for career-oriented programs at the university[40] is reflected in the emphasis of campus library collections on business, computer science, criminal justice, and health science materials, depending upon the academic programs offered on the campus. At the two smaller branch campus libraries, support for programs offered on the campus ranges from minimal to barely adequate.[41] At the Dickinson campus library, the collection is small but developing to support the programs currently offered at that branch, primarily library science, public health administration, business, and education. At the Hawthorne campus, the library's collection is larger with an emphasis upon business, but dependent upon the nearby Emerson campus library.

As campuses increasingly share programs, it will become necessary for the libraries to be given additional funding to develop, at the least, core collections to support new programs on each campus. The Emerson campus senior vice-president/university provost, in response to a proposal made by the faculty library committee on campus, has within the past year inaugurated a policy of giving funds to the library to buy materials in advance or during the establishment of a new program.[42] This should augur new university support for all libraries now that the position of university director of libraries has been established and this policy can be expanded.

Before the reorganization of the university, system-wide academic planning was nonexistent, with inconsistent representation by a library director on the council of deans of each campus. Since this is the first year of the reorganization, the libraries for the first time are involved in central academic planning; for example, a new telecommunications program is being offered at the Thoreau and the Emerson campuses, with the dean responsible for the program determining what will be needed at each campus. To facilitate those decisions he will confer with the university director of libraries.[43] Another ex-

Institution II (Clemens University)

ample is the sharing of the pharmacy collection of the college of pharmacy in the Thoreau campus with the library at the Emerson campus as pharmacy courses will now be offered there also.

To provide resources across the entire system for cooperative multicampus degrees and programs, the Emerson campus library has shared library materials with other campus libraries. Resource identification and selection are facilitated by computer terminals at Dickinson, Hawthorne and Cooper linked to the Emerson campus library. A courier system is used for delivery of routine interlibrary loans among the campuses and for the delivery of subject areas to support a particular program for which the requesting campus library has inadequate materials. Such resource sharing has crossed the regional divisions, as when Emerson (in the eastern region) sent to the Dickinson campus library (in the western region) Hebraic materials for a program and library science materials for reserve assignments.

The dispersion of some programs among campuses will affect campus libraries in ways yet to be worked out, although many programs will continue to be registered only with individual campuses. Both the Thoreau campus and the Emerson campus have distinctly different inventories of programs registered with the state department of education. Master's programs continue to be unique to each campus; the only Ph.D. program offered at the university is at the Thoreau campus. Although library support of new programs has varied, programs that must be approved by the state department of education to be registered with a specified campus involve the library at the campus level, as the state requires a report on the library's holdings, including the number of volumes, number of periodical titles, budget available to develop programs, and the projected budget required to support the program.[44]

Although encouraged on all campuses, faculty participation in the development of collections varies from campus to campus. Ultimately, selection is made by the professional staff within library budgets. When additional monies were allocated to the Cooper campus, faculty were promptly contacted to submit requests for new items they would want available. The use of Choice cards by the staff in all the campus libraries is common, frequently with assignment of specific areas to specific librarians.

No multicampus coordinated collection development policy exists. Consideration is given by each campus library to programs that have a high priority, the types of programs served, and the differing costs of materials by disciplines. Although resources are allocated within each campus library primarily on the basis of assessment of current needs, only in the Emerson campus library is an acquisitions policy used with levels of collecting based upon a formula. The formula is one evolved by the acquisitions librarian at the Emerson library for the allocation of funds by subject based upon enrollment statistics, circulation statistics, number of majors in the subjects, number of graduate students in the subjects, and number of faculty in the various departments. The formula has not been applied to periodicals allocation; that budget is not divided by subject. Special effort is made by the Emerson campus library to support new programs. As an example, after evaluating the collection it was determined that the new paralegal program required the purchase of an additional $14,000 of materials; the funds were taken from their supply line.

Institution II (Clemens University)   133

  The other campus libraries do not use a formula, relying instead upon historical precedent. The chief of the Cooper campus library, for example, has found that dividing the book budget by assigning percentages by subject has not worked very well; he therefore allocates funds based upon the library's assessment of current needs. Cost is often a deciding factor, since marine science books, science periodicals, art books and periodicals are significantly more expensive than books in the humanities, social sciences, and business. The library weighs the cost of a book against its availability from other campuses, how many courses are given in that area and therefore how many students will use the book, as well as what the current collection already has in that subject area.

  At the Thoreau campus library, the chief appointed a collection development committee to draft collection development statements concerning gifts, documents, and AV materials. With that document, the committee completely revised and reevaluated the list of continuations. Due to a limited book budget, faculty and library staff have had little discretionary funds for enrichment of the collection; the Thoreau library confines the greatest share of purchases to support areas perceived to have the highest priority and to new programs being started on campus.[45]

  At the Longfellow branch, which uses the library of the host college, the library director stated that through the university relationship with his college and the funds derived from that partnership, his library has grown in depth and breadth of subject collections. As the university has offered additional areas of graduate study, the library has responded by developing the collection to supply the needs of the graduate students. To accomplish this, the director works with the Clemens university coordinators of graduate departments. (However, no contact at all has occurred until this time between the director and any of the libraries of the university.)

Projected changes in the budget process will mandate university-wide purchasing. At present, there is no centralized university policy for the purchase of library materials and library equipment; they are purchased by the individual libraries. However, purchase of other equipment such as chairs, furniture, carpeting, etc. is carried out through a central purchasing agent in the office of the vice-president of finance, provided such purchases have been factored into the budget of the requesting campus.

Personnel Policies

Librarians have faculty status as members of the campus unions with personnel policies relating to promotion requirements, staff development, pay scales, benefits and appeals generally uniform for all the multicampus libraries, despite the fact that the Thoreau, Emerson, and Cooper campuses have different union contracts, with separate unions for full-time and part-time faculty on the Emerson campus.[46] As a result of a strike by the faculty at Thoreau, there now is pay equity between the Emerson and Thoreau campuses. The last union contract at the Thoreau campus provided for more vacation time plus the same full faculty status with professional rank for the library staff as is enjoyed by the Emerson campus.[47]

Promotion requirements for librarians are the same in all unions. A university-wide policy stipulates that thirty credits beyond the MLS are required for professorial rank. However, the criteria used by each personnel committee or chief to determine recommendations for promotion are not uniform. In the Emerson campus library initial appointment, reappointment, promotion and tenure are reviewed by a personnel committee of seven librarians elected for two-year overlapping terms. Recommendations are then submitted to the Centralized Promotion and Tenure Board before going to the library chief. The Emerson campus librarians have a ten-month contract, while the Cooper campus librarians have an eleven-month contract. A new contract in the Fall of 1986 may equalize this.

Librarians can not move with relative ease from a position in one library to another in a different region within the system. Such job movement is unlikely, as librarians in eastern campus libraries belong to a different union than those in western region libraries. However, there is some precedent for moves within a region: the director of the Dickinson campus library had been a librarian in the Thoreau campus library; the director of the Hawthorne library and his assistant had been members of the Emerson campus library.

Library Budget Process

The university budget is approximately $102 million; the total of all libraries' budgets represents approximately 3% of this total. This does not mean that the same proportion holds true for each library's share of its campus budget. According to the senior vice-president/university provost of the Emerson campus, the campus spends approximately 5% of its budget on the library, including salaries and computer.[48] The chief of the library of that campus stated that the figure approaches 4%, although in different categories it has been as high as 4.7%. One year the amount approached 5% when the campus experienced a tremendous influx of students and, concommitantly, a large increase in the budget. At the Cooper campus the under-support of the library is demonstrated by a ratio that ranges from 1%-2% of the campus budget, with 2.5% maximum. At the Thoreau campus the most recent ratio of library expenditures was 2.4%.

All libraries have control of their budgets both in preparation and expenditure. However, established salary lines cannot be changed as they are governed by contractual agreements or by the administration's ability to make lines available. While it is within the purview of the chief of the Emerson campus library, for example, to move funds, if needed, from the library materials line to support part-time positions, approval is required to move funds from the salary line to the materials line. Under no circumstances can the fund for capital outlay be invaded.

No uniform library budgetary system is followed. The process for planning, developing, and administering the annual budget has varied from library to library. Guidelines for the annual university budget are developed initially by the board of trustees each year. The board may establish, for example, a flat percentage of increase or the requirement for a substantial justification for new staff appointments. The chief of the Emerson campus library (with the largest budget of any of the libraries) distributes copies of the guidelines to each of his department heads for their recommendations. Department heads then initiate requests for materials and supplies; as many as possible are filled. (Unfilled requests are resubmitted the following year.) After individual discussions by the campus chief with the department heads, a unified budget request is submitted to the senior vice-president/university provost of the eastern division. After a series of meetings during which the budgets are analyzed (without the presence of the campus

Institution II (Clemens University)　　　　　　137

library chief), with the senior vice-president defending them before the university center, they are submitted to the board of trustees for approval.

The Thoreau campus library has not enjoyed a budget process. In previous years the budget for the campus library had been presented to the library chief as an accomplished fact. It varied slightly year to year, changing by plus or minus $5,000. This procedure had virtually been ordained by steady revenue losses by the campus for the past decade. Improved circumstances this year enabled the procedure to be modified; for the first time, the chief was asked to originate and submit budget requests and support them with justifications and rationale.

For Cooper the budget requests and justifications were submitted this year to the chief of the Emerson campus library with copies to the provost of Cooper campus. The chief of the Emerson campus library conveyed it to the administration. In prior years the budget request had been submitted to the campus provost who reviewed it in the context of other budget requests on the campus, and then presented a total package to the senior vice-president/university provost of the Emerson Campus. He, in turn, submitted it to the university center.

The budgets of the Cooper and the Thoreau campus libraries have been insufficient for years, as is acknowledged by the current administration. With the current division of the university into eastern and western regions, it is possible to shift appropriated funds only among the campus libraries within the eastern region. Since the intent was announced in 1983 to merge administratively the Cooper campus with the Emerson campus and the Emerson campus became responsible for Cooper's library, the Emerson campus library chief authorized an allotment of funds to strengthen the library recognized by all as inadequate, and increased its expenditures for library materials by one-third each year for the following three years.

The degree of support given to libraries in the eastern region has not been enjoyed by the western region. The Thoreau campus has not provided the library with adequate resources and funds to support new programs, nor has the library been included early in the planning for such new programs. As support for the Thoreau campus library deteriorated in the early 1970s, maintenance of its collections eroded; the library, while housed in an attractive new building, has a smaller budget, a smaller staff, and a smaller collection than the Emerson campus library, even though it supports the only Ph.D. program in the university.

In some years the university has had to rescind portions of the library budgets, the amount varying from campus to campus.[49] In its "Report on the Survey of the [Emerson] Campus Library" the Library Visiting Committee gave priority to the need for a stabilized budget for the Emerson campus library which would "give the Library administration an opportunity to plan in an orderly and economic way the best use of the available funds."[50] Yet that library has fared better than the Thoreau campus library, both in its acquisitions budget for new materials and in its periodicals budget; recent years have brought increases across the board of 5-10%. Consequently, the Emerson campus library is larger in size, collection, and staff than the two other large campus libraries.

In the president's announcement of the new position of university director of libraries, he stated: "The new system ... in other cases ... will mean transferring budget

Institution II (Clemens University)

lines to bolster acquisitions."[51] The new university director of libraries has been given the prerogative to shift budgets from one part of the system to another should that become necessary or desirable, even though the budgets are campus derived. It is assumed that library budgets will remain campus based, as are the budgets of the university deans.

Cooperation and Resource Sharing

Within both the eastern region and the western region are resource sharing opportunities with other libraries, both academic, special, and public. In the eastern region, all colleges and universities are members of a regional cooperative resource council. Funded by the state to assist libraries in the council in borrowing from each other, a courier service makes deliveries three days a week. This service is used constantly by the Emerson and Cooper campus libraries for interlibrary loan purposes. The regional cooperative resource council is used by the Cooper library more often for interlibrary loan with other academic libraries than for direct request to the campus libraries of the university. Government documents collections in the region have an active cooperative arrangement and use the same courier service to exchange materials and to provide delivery of wanted materials to each of the twelve depository members. About ten years ago the depositories of two major counties developed a cooperative acquisition plan to assume responsibility for collections in specific areas of publication.

In addition, several county library networks exist for cooperative purposes and for resource sharing. Even though some members are competitive academic institutions their library staff meet three to four times a year and call upon one another for requests outside the normal interlibrary loan channels. The Clemens university staff have closer contact with members of the networks than with the Thoreau or Cooper campus library staff.

Six academic libraries in the area of the Thoreau campus library have formed an association which publishes a union list of serials for their use. The Thoreau campus library uses that microfiche list for selection purposes as well as for interlibrary loan. With an ID card, students of each member institution have free access to the other libraries but with some restrictions on borrowing. The member libraries are very close geographically with no one library more than a brief walking distance from the other libraries. The students of the Thoreau campus library constantly use the local business branch of the public library system for their assignments as it, too, is within walking distance of the campus and is far superior in resources to their campus library. Students also have convenient access to the main branch of the public library. For health science students, a regional medical library not far from the campus is available. The Thoreau campus library is a member of a metropolitan consortia which admits faculty, students, and staff of the campus to the resources of academic and special libraries in the vast metropolitan area. (That membership also qualifies the library for some state aid for academic libraries.)

Intercampus communication among the multicampus libraries of the university varies. In the eastern region both Hawthorne and Cooper have contact with the Emerson campus, with Hawthorne much more frequently. The Hawthorne librarian attends all department head meetings at the Emerson campus and is considered a member of their staff. While the Dickinson campus library has been reassigned to the western region, its interli-

Institution II (Clemens University)

brary loan activities and other contacts continue to be with the Emerson campus library in the eastern region. Very little intercampus communication exists between the east and west regions; although some of this is due to the geographic distances, it is for the most part because of an historic pattern of insularity. The strained relationships that have existed between the Thoreau and Emerson campuses have been reflected in the libraries. Currently there is little interaction among the staffs of the two: no meetings, no sharing of common problems among those in similar positions, no sharing of information, no sharing of periodical lists. The statement of the coordinator of public services of the Thoreau campus library is revealing: "I never call the reference department at [Emerson] campus; I don't even know who the librarians are at [Emerson] campus; I don't know what their collection is. I know the librarians at [neighboring library] well. If we need something, we call one of the people around here."[52] As a long-time Thoreau campus librarian he feels that hostility has always existed between the two campuses, probably, to his thinking, because of the resentment by the Thoreau campus that it had been the parent campus and now the Emerson campus is bigger and richer.[53]

While policies of the multicampus libraries permit access to all university students, the geographical distances make this likelihood remote. Indeed, the university's libraries maintain an open access policy to everyone. The merits of this policy, however, currently are being reassessed by the university administration at the request of the Emerson campus library,[54] as the policy is proving a problem to its periodicals department and the center for business research. The open door policy has resulted in extensive use by high school students and the community, especially of the center for business research library.⁵⁵ This has aggravated staffing and security problems, particularly during evenings, weekends, and vacations. Two neighboring professional schools pay a yearly subsidy to the Emerson campus to help defray costs for the use their students make of the library.

Technical Services and Automation

No system-wide policies for technical services, reference services, or bibliographic control exist to guide the administration of library services. There is no system-wide mission and goals statement, nor, actually, written policy of any kind. The 1982 Middle States Association report included a recommendation to the Emerson campus library to prepare written policies, a recommendation not yet carried out.⁵⁶

Planning for an online circulation system and catalog has been notable only at the Emerson campus library. A major step in establishing system-wide library standards at the university is the recent adoption of automation networking, which requires standardization and uniformity in hardware and procedures by all participating campuses in the eastern region. Initiated by the chief of the Emerson campus library, the system is developing and has the strong support of the president of the university. Starting in 1979 the chief of that library obtained grant funds for an online system, purchased equipment for his library, and obtained equipment for the branch campus libraries in his region. Using his library as the host, he has formed a library network to share the various subsystems of the Emerson campus library's CLSI library management system. The goal is to develop a multi-type library network extending beyond the university libraries to academic, governmental, high school and special research libraries in the region. This

Institution II (Clemens University)   143

system when complete will provide automated acquisitions, circulation, serials control, non-print media control and an online catalog. At this time only the Emerson campus library and the libraries of Cooper, Hawthorne, and Dickinson are actively entering their collections into the database. Since September 1984 the Emerson campus library has ceased producing catalog cards, relying instead upon its online catalog. The administration recognizes the importance of the system in helping Cooper, Dickinson, and Hawthorne, all of whose collections are small; their limitations are mitigated by their ability to access the more extensive holdings of the Emerson campus library. The online system is currently funded from the Emerson campus budget; when it becomes university-wide, it will become part of the university center budget with proportional charges assessed against the individual campuses.[57]

The Thoreau campus library had no terminal to connect to the network at the time of this research, nor had funds been committed to a retrospective conversion of its records for the university database. Due to an inadequate library equipment budget, it was only in 1982, through a gift from campus alumni, that an OCLC terminal was acquired by the library.

The new president, at the time of his announcement of a university-wide library system, stated:

> In the long run, however, the need is ... for the expansion of all the collections and of our capacity to access those collections from any [university] site. For this reason, concommitant with the creation of the new library system ... our goal is to find the needed financial wherewithal to link completely the campuses: from user-ac-

cess terminals to courier services, to facsimile systems.[58]

Summary

Clemens University is a private, nonsectarian multicampus university with six campuses, an example of a consolidated system with no significantly large main campus --an aggregation under a central administration. Widely dispersed geographically, the greatest distance between two campuses is over 100 miles. With a current total enrollment of approximately 20,000 students and over 1,000 full-time and part-time faculty, the university offers over 300 undergraduate and graduate degree programs by eight faculties, six of them across all campuses.

The university expanded from its original urban campus to five suburban campuses after World War II, in response to population shifts and to the demand by returning veterans for higher education. The pattern of growth is similar to other multicampus institutions responding to a declining urban environment and a concommitant growth of population in suburban regions. Of the six campuses, three are large campuses which are owned by the university and with a resident faculty; three smaller campuses are in rented facilities with no resident faculty. Clemens University has experienced considerable change in organization, governance, and administrative positions during its history. Each main campus had operated almost completely autonomously under campus administrators who considered each campus the equivalent to an independent college.

The student population differs in each of the major campuses; the urban (Thoreau) campus has a higher percentage of minority and lower income level students, while the

Institution II (Clemens University)

suburban campuses (Emerson and Cooper) have predominantly middle class students and a larger part-time adult population. However, common to all campuses is a large number of first-generation college students.

The university has demonstrated a creative and entrepreneurial approach in reaching out to students not already enrolled on the three large campuses. It has entered into a partnership with a private undergraduate college in a wealthy county (Longfellow County) to provide graduate programs on their facility and share the expenses or losses. The university in two instances when creating a branch campus (Dickinson and Longfellow) sited the programs on the grounds of an existing college and entered into a contract with the resident campus to provide instant library support. Dickinson and Longfellow then could immediately display for accreditation a library already in place for the graduate programs offered. In a third instance, the university created Hawthorne campus as a "coordinate campus" --unique in that it combined an urban parochial college and the suburban campus programs on the grounds of a convent.[59] In all three cases branches developed as a matter of expediency where a library already existed.

At the Thoreau campus, the development of the Emerson campus was perceived as draining the Thoreau campus when that campus was the principal revenue generator. Yet today, after twelve years of deficits, the Thoreau campus would likely not exist were it not for the income generated by the Emerson campus. The two campus libraries reflect this state. The library that was created at the Emerson campus twenty years ago was already larger and better equiped ten years later than the Thoreau campus library, creating resentment that still can be detected today. Resolution of the Thoreau library's needs cannot continue to be deferred. A report issued by two consultants in August 1985 summarizes its current problems and urges the university and campus administration to provide the Thoreau campus library in the immediate future with "appropriate support and appropriate visibility ..." in order to produce a more valuable library.[60]

With the current administrative and organizational change from a federated system to a centralized administration under a new president, the libraries too are in the process of organizational and administrative change. The appointment of a university director of libraries by the president is intended to overcome the autonomy of each of the libraries under the previous federated system of campuses and will be a major factor in drawing the university together into a unified institution. The local needs of campus libraries often became subordinated to the needs of the central organization. As a result, budget support for individual collection building was sometimes insufficient. To compensate for this, the administration expected the Emerson campus library to share its resources with the smaller libraries or to provide materials through intercampus loans.

A priority of the chief of the Emerson campus library (who is now the university director of libraries) is to tie all campus libraries into the Emerson campus library database as speedily as possible, and then expand the database so that each campus will know what the others have. This will involve a major undertaking of retrospective conversion at the Thoreau and Cooper campuses. The computerization and database will be the keys to the success of sharing resources among the campuses within the university. Technological developments are expected to have considerable impact upon the multicampus library

Institution II (Clemens University)

system as telecommunication and computerization encourage resource sharing, including identification and transportation of resources from one campus to another.

One of the vexing concerns of this multicampus university is the inordinate amount of time used by administrators in traveling between campuses whose geographical span is so great (well over a hundred miles between the two furthest campuses). The annual cost of a continuing program of gathering the various library staffs together for meetings would be staggering. The frequency with which a university director of libraries can visit each campus is questionable, as is the bringing together of all campus library chiefs and department heads in management meetings.

It is principally the geographical distances which have resulted in the various units taking on a life of their own, independent of the university. As the campuses functioned as autonomous units, so did the libraries of those campuses. Distances encouraged provincialism, with faculty and staff failing to understand that campuses and libraries are part of the same university, with growth or retrenchment as one university, not as individual campuses and libraries.

The history of the university and of two major campus libraries is unusually intertwined, probably more than in many other institutions, due to the strong personalities of two successive library chiefs of the Thoreau campus. The first librarian, who was viewed as an empire builder,[61] involved the campus in political turmoil for years as he made the construction of the new library building a political issue. In addition to being campus library director, he headed the art department and the university press, was dean for campus planning, and undertook other academic responsibilities. His assistant and then successor continued the separate kingdom concept. This was, in part, responsible for the lack of support given the library by an antagonized faculty. Within the Thoreau campus library itself, each of the departments remained separate and aloof; departments contacted the chief only, with little communication and no cooperation among them.

The first chief of the Thoreau campus library resented the fact that after founding the Emerson campus library, and later the Cooper library, he was removed from the responsibility over them when the Emerson campus became a free-standing campus with a librarian reporting to the senior officer of that campus.[62] During those years the central administration of the university was located on the Thoreau campus, which was then the flagship campus. This increased the responsibility of the library chief of Thoreau as he was involved in university and multicampus planning until the federated model for the university was instituted.

On the Emerson campus the library has also been an important part of the campus, and again due to the strong personality of the original chief librarian. He had a close rapport with the first and second presidents of the Emerson campus (as the campus administrator was then called), as well as being one of the original five faculty who governed the campus. A very aggressive man, he demanded and obtained full consideration for the library from the very beginning. That has continued to be a tradition on the Emerson campus. Due to his persistance and perseverance, the fourth or fifth building constructed on the campus was the present library building, still the largest single building and occupying one of the most prominent locations. It is this historic support

Institution II (Clemens University)

of the library which is responsible for its growth from a one-room library with four staff members to a full-service library with over seventy professional and nonprofessional staff.

While the history of library support at Emerson campus was strong from the very beginning, the opposite has been true of Cooper. There the history is one of deferred maintenance and inadequate resources. Significant deficits and turmoil in administration of the college have had an impact on the library during the nineteen years the present library chief has been there. While he is of the opinion that its record of small library budgets and inadequate building and resources may be changed by the university-wide library system now being developed, the library may be sacrificing some of its local decision-making, an ever-present trade-off in multi-campus institutions.

Notes

[1] The senior vice-president/university provost of the Emerson campus noted that there are really three kinds of campuses at the university: 1) two which could stand alone; 2) satellite campuses which can not possibly stand on their own; and 3) a small, full campus which can almost stand on its own. Interview July 12, 1985.

[2] "Recommendations for the Organization and Structure of [Clemens] University," Prepared by _____, December 30, 1970. (Typewritten), p. 3.

[3] Self-Study [Clemens] University the [Thoreau] Center, Fall 1982, p. 15. Under the federated structure the Thoreau campus and the Emerson campus prepared their own self-studies for Middle States accreditation.

4 Interview with the chief of the Thoreau library, July 2, 1985.

5 "[Clemens] University's 1984 Institutional Master Plan," Submitted February 12, 1985 by the Deputy President to the Deputy Commissioner for Higher and Professional Education. (Typewritten).

6 "Report to [Clemens] University, University Center ... by An Evaluation Team Representing the Commission on Higher Education of the Middle States Association of Colleges and Schools, Prepared after Study of the Institution's Follow-Up Report and a Visit to the University Center on November 11-13, 1984." (Typewritten), p. 2.

7 "[Clemens] University/[Thoreau] Campus. Library Development Program Proposal," n.d. (Typewritten), p. 1.

8 "In 1968, only 11% of our students came from Black and Hispanic backgrounds; during the next five years the percentage increased to 27%; currently, 65% of our 4378 undergrduates are Black or Hispanic." Ibid.

9 "[Clemens] University's 1984 Institutional Master Plan," p. 7.

10 The term "matrix management" came into prominence in the 1960s in the defense industry. Today, it is used to imply "... an overlay of horizontal authority and responsibility relationships on top of a functional structure .... The professionals and supervisors working in such an environment must accustom themselves to dual authority and a dual information and reporting system." Dale S. Beach, Personnel: the Management of People at Work, 5th ed. (New York: Macmillan, 1985), pp. 71-72.

Institution II (Clemens University)　　　　　151

[11] According to the senior vice-president/ university provost of the Thoreau campus, the university deans cut across the entire university and report to him concerning budgets, operations, but report directly to the president on long-range matters. He supervises three of the university deans for the president; the senior vice-president/university provost of the Emerson campus supervises the other two. Interview with the senior vice-president/university provost of the Thoreau campus, July 12, 1985.

[12] The position of vice-president for academic affairs was posted in the summer of 1986. Before the creation of university faculties, each of the two major regions had a vice-president for academic affairs, an office created in 1973 to whom the deans of the various schools on each campus reported.

[13] Letter dated November 17, 1983 from the chancellor. (Typewritten).

[14] "Section 2. Campus Nomenclature: All campuses, branches and extensions shall bear the name [Clemens] University with a local or regional designation; e.g., [Clemens] University at [Thoreau] campus ..." in "Chapter II: Organization of the University," [Clemens] University Statutes, 24 January 1984, p. 13.

[15] "Report to [Clemens] University, University Center ... by An Evaluation Team Representing the Commission on Higher Education of the Middle States Association of Colleges and Schools, Prepared after Study of the Institution's Self-Study Report and a Visit to the University Center on January 23 to January 25, 1983." (Typewritten), p. 15.

[16] [Clemens] University Financial Report 1983-1984, p. 3.

[17] Interview with the university dean for academic planning and evaluation, June 7, 1985.

[18] Self-Study Report of [Emerson] Center of [Clemens] University, 1982, p. 151.

[19] Ibid., p. 158.

[20] Less than $5,000,000, according to the vice-president of finance and treasurer, June 20, 1985.

[21] Ibid.

[22] Interview with the university dean for academic planning and evaluation, June 7, 1985.

[23] A significant part of unrestricted revenue (4.7% in 1984, 5.3% in 1983, 5.7% in 1982) is provided by the state's program of direct aid to private higher education. [Clemens] University Financial Report 1983-1984, p. 5.

[24] In an interview with the dean of communications, computer and information science, August 8, 1985, he stated that at least 50% of the university's students are dependent upon federal and state aid, combined with guaranteed student loans.

[25] "Celebrating the 25th Anniversary of [Emerson] Center 1954-1979," Summit 4 (September 1979): 28.

[26] "Report to the Faculty, Administration, Trustees of [Emerson] Center of [Clemens] University ... by An Evaluation Team Representing the Commission on Higher Education of the Middle States Association of Colleges and Schools, Prepared after Study of the Institution's Self-Study Report and a Visit to the Campus of [Emerson] October 24-27, 1982." (Typewritten), p. 1.

Institution II (Clemens University)

[27] Interview with the provost of the Cooper campus, August 2, 1985.

[28] "Goals Set for [Cooper] Campus," _____ 31 March 1986, sec. B, p. 2.

[29] "[Clemens] University [Thoreau] Campus Library: A Report 1981-1985," _____, Director of the Library, July 1985. (Typewritten), p. 2.

[30] The library chief of the Thoreau campus library reported to the dean of instructional resources: "For purposes of shared automation, we are better off attempting to create a [university] library system. It is cheaper and more efficient to build on [Emerson's and Cooper's] efforts than to create a new network with just [the school under investigation] and [Thoreau] Center." "Memorandum," March 15, 1983. (Typewritten), p. 4.

[31] "[Emerson] Library Faculty Minutes of Meeting, September 21, 1984." (Typewritten), p. 1.

[32] In the "Memorandum of Understanding between the [Thoreau Campus], [Clemens] University and ... College," it states: "Five percent of program revenues shall be allocated for direct library acquisitions in support of [Clemens] University's graduate programs at ... College." <u>Self-Study [Clemens] University, the [Thoreau] Center</u>, Appendix 25, p. 6.

[33] Interview with the chief of the Thoreau campus library July 2, 1985.

[34] Interview with the dean of instructional resources, Thoreau campus, July 23, 1985.

[35] Instructional resources had been created in 1977, consisting of the library, special

academic services, and the communications center, to bring together "those campus resources that directly support the academic curricula without their being traditional academic programs ..." "Self-Study [Clemens] University, the [Thoreau] Center," p. 100.

[36] "Report on the Survey of the ... Library of the [Emerson] College Center," April 1977. (Typewritten), p. 5.

[37] "Memorandum For: The Library Faculty and Staff of [Clemens] University; From: _____, President; Subject: The Creation of a University-Wide Library System," July 29, 1985. (Typewritten).

[38] Interview with the provost of the Hawthorne campus, June 28, 1985.

[39] "University Task Force - Libraries," October 19, 1983. (Typewritten), p. 1

[40] "With few exceptions, students enrolling at [Clemens] do so with strong career intent; the vast majority attend college in order to secure the specific skills and credentials requisite for employment." "[Clemens] University's 1984 Institutional Master Plan," p. 7.

[41] A report of the Middle States Team commented: "Library collections at [Hawthorne and Dickinson] were found to be very small, although courier service and reserve materials placement combine to provide current adequacy. Systematic attention to increasing these collections should be of prime concern." In "Report to the Faculty, Administration, Trustees of [Emerson] Center of [Clemens] University ... by An Evaluation Team Representing the Commission on Higher Education of the Middle States Association of Colleges and Schools," p. 11.

Institution II (Clemens University)　　　　155

⁴² "[Emerson] Library Faculty Minutes of Meeting, April 26, 1985." (Typewritten), p. 1.

⁴³ Interview with the dean of communications, computer and information science, August 8, 1985.

⁴⁴ The head of the Thoreau campus library stated that the same materials are used over and over again for various programs, and that the campus has been denied accreditation for programs (i.e., a Doctorate in Professional Studies for Counselors) because the library resources can not support them. Interview with the chief of the Thoreau campus library, July 21, 1985.

⁴⁵ "The [Thoreau] Campus Library has the additional problem of needing to serve an extraordinary diverse group of students: psychology doctoral students, chemistry and business master's students, the traditional undergraduate and the struggling, motivated, but unprepared and semi-literate freshman." "[Clemens] University [Thoreau] Campus Library: A Report 1981-1985," pp. 5-6.

⁴⁶ In an interview with a member of the board of trustees, July 11, 1985, he stated that the board would hope to see at some point one union for the whole university; however, he conceded that might not be good as the union would have too much power.

⁴⁷ The Emerson campus union contract agreement reads: "INCLUDED: All full-time professors, associate professors, assistant professors, instructors, professional librarians, department chairman, guidance counselors, and research associates ..." Agreement Between [Clemens] University and the [Emerson] Collegial Federation ... September 1, 1980 to August 31, 1985, p. 2.

⁴⁸ Interview with the senior vice-president/university provost of the Emerson campus, June 7, 1985. He was unable to measure the expenditures for Hawthorne since all services at Hawthorne are underwritten by the Emerson campus.

⁴⁹ "We have gone from zero book budgets to substantial ones; we have been on a yo-yo for ten or fifteen years, and it would be nice to have a two or three year spell of adequacy in budget and staff." Interview with the chief of the Cooper campus library, August 2, 1985.

⁵⁰ "Report on the Survey of the ... Library of the [Emerson] College Center," April 1977. (Typewritten), pp. 4-5.

⁵¹ "Memorandum For: The Library Faculty and Staff of [Clemens] University; From: _____, President; Subject: The Creation of a University-Wide Library System," July 29, 1985. (Typewritten).

⁵² Interview with the coordinator of public services, Thoreau campus library, July 28, 1985.

⁵³ Ibid. This resentment has been expressed by one of the first library chiefs: "When we acquired [Emerson] ... it was [...] who inaugurated library services which I carried on under his supervision. [Emerson's] first full-time Librarian ... was hired ... on my recommendation.... [As to] the opening of [Cooper] ... I purchased 14,000 volumes for them, organized their first library .... So, as you can see, [we] served all the University libraries, not just those here in [Thoreau]." "Annual Report - A Personal Note; ... My Final Annual Library Report to the President (of Thoreau campus), October 9, 1980." (Typewritten), p. 2.

Institution II (Clemens University)　　　　　157

[54] "Over the summer 60% using the library are non [Clemens] University." Interview with the executive assistant to the president, October 2, 1985.

[55] The senior vice-president/university provost of the Emerson campus also has expressed reservations about continuing the open access policy. Interview June 7, 1985.

[56] "A final recommendation to improve long-range planning for library collection and resources ... written policies to serve as objectives in the areas of selection and discarding of materials ..." "Report to the Faculty, Administration, Trustees of [Emerson] Center of [Clemens] University ... by An Evaluation Team Representing the Commission on Higher Education of the Middle States Association of Colleges and Schools," pp. 11-12.

[57] Interview with the vice-president for finance and treasurer, June 21, 1985.

[58] "Memorandum For: The Library Faculty and Staff of [Clemens] University; From:＿＿＿＿＿, President; Subject: The Creation of a University-Wide Library System," July 29, 1985. (Typewritten).

[59] This was the only coordinate campus the state has ever had. It lasted for approximately ten years until the parochial college moved away to larger quarters. During its presence, the parochial college offered liberal arts and science courses; Clemens University taught professional courses: business, accounting, criminal justice, computer science, etc. An upper division program only, at the same graduation ceremony people graduated from two colleges.

[60] "A Consideration of the Condition of the [Clemens] University [Thoreau] Center Li-

brary," Prepared by _____, August, 1985. (Typewritten), p. 8. In the report the consultants address the problems of "outdated information, limited staff and the atmosphere of neglect." p. 1.

[61] Interview with the coordinator of public services, Thoreau campus, July 28, 1985.

[62] The librarian had the title of university librarian and director of libraries in the Thoreau campus. He had actually physically brought the books out to the Emerson campus and established the library there before the Emerson librarian was hired. Interview with the vice-president for finance and treasurer, June 21, 1985.

CHAPTER IV

INSTITUTION III (CHASE UNIVERSITY)

A. THE ENVIRONMENT: THE UNIVERSITY AND ITS SETTING

Background and Description

With approximately 25,000 full-time and part-time day and evening students, 1,600 faculty, nine schools and three major campuses, Chase University (Institution III), located in the Northeast, offers over 200 registered programs in associate, baccalaureate, masters, and doctoral programs. A privately supported institution, it functions under the direction of a board of trustees.[1] The university is committed "to providing a balance between career and life preparation,"[2] and, as such, has grown to be the second largest independent university in the state, as well as ranking in 1984 among the ten largest independent universities nationwide in total student enrollment.[3]

Chase University is located on three campuses (see figure 10), one, the Dupont campus, on a two-and-a-half acre site in the financial district of a major city, not far from the university's original setting of 1906. The other two campuses, Kodak and Bethlehem/Kellog, are close to one another, Bethlehem/Kellog on over two hundred acres in a suburban residental area and the Kodak campus in two locations in a county seat. No more than twenty minutes drive from each

Multicampus Libraries

Distances are approximate

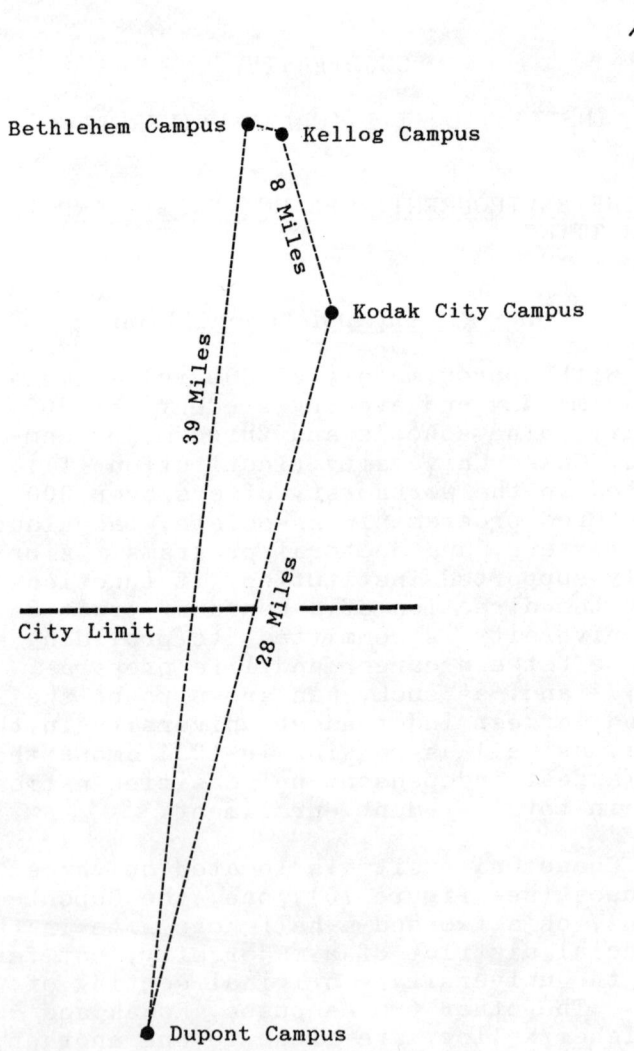

Figure 10
CHASE UNIVERSITY
DISTANCES BETWEEN CAMPUSES BY AUTO ROUTE

other, both campuses are in Fairchild county, an hour's drive from the Dupont campus.

Chase University began as a proprietary venture, a specialized institute dedicated to instruction in professional accountancy. Two brothers from Ohio, one a certified public accountant and the other an attorney, borrowed on an insurance policy and formed a new business school for accountants in 1906. The first class had thirteen students (ten men and three women), meeting two nights a week in one classroom. Because of the risks involved in the new venture, one brother continued for several years to hold his job as the corporate secretary of a railway.

In addition to classes held in rented space in an office building in the financial section, the school began to offer evening courses in YMCAs in the home city and in a neighboring city; in very short time the school was offering courses in four locations. The brothers taught the courses and wrote the textbooks: the lawyer wrote the business law texts and the certified public accountant the accounting texts. As the enrollment grew, the faculty grew; soon in more than fifty cities around the country evening extension courses were taught. The third president described the university's upward climb:

> In the years before World War II [Chase] was a chain operation, with 43 branches throughout the country .... As the operation grew, it became more and more difficult for the ... brothers to travel around the country to all their outposts. So they converted to a franchise operation, with branch managers as owners. All of them were obliged to purchase their text books from the brothers...[4]

In the metropolitan city where they held their first class, locations changed several times as the need for more space arose. They moved first to larger quarters in the same area, remaining there for fourteen years, then to another location where they remained until 1953, and finally, as the Dupont campus, to a sixteen-story building which the university still owns and uses.

In 1919 Chase University began offering a day program in accountancy and business administration in addition to the evening courses, partially in response to the federal government's rehabilitation programs for disabled veterans of World War I. The emphasis upon accounting and business continued as the institute established schools for major fields of instruction: a school of accountancy and business administration; a school of marketing, advertising and selling; and a school of shorthand and secretarial practice. Although still a business school, the institute began to add courses in English, mathematics, and social sciences.

In 1942 a son of one of the founding brothers became the second president of the institute. The family, however, surrendered to the school all claim to assets which amounted to approximately $1 million.[5] Thus the institution, which operated on a non-profit basis from 1935, officially achieved non-profit status in 1947.[6] In December 1948, the state board of regents granted the institute collegiate status, with the right to confer upon graduates of the college the bachelor of business administration degree. Chase promptly began to expand the courses offered to other areas of study.

In 1950 the college established a school of arts and sciences with its own curricula and faculty; as a result, the board of regents in 1953 granted the college approval to

Institution III (Chase University)

confer the bachelor of arts degree. Accreditation by the Middle States Association of Colleges and Secondary Schools was granted in 1956. This was followed in 1958 with approval by the board of regents to offer a master of business administration degree. The business programs were successful due in large part to the enrollment of the many veterans returning to school under the G.I. Bill of Rights.

In 1960 the second president of the institution, after an association with the school for thirty-six years, resigned. The board of trustees elected as the third president his long-time associate since 1947, a man who had been assistant dean, dean, then provost, and vice-president. In March 1973 the board of regents of the state informed the president of the college that its petition to be designated a university had been approved. Thus, through a relatively brief period of time, the institution progressed from a business institute to a college to a multicampus university offering diversified undergraduate and graduate programs.

The number of schools increased by 1986 to a total of eight schools at four locations organized under university deans: graduate school of business (1963), school of education (1966), school of nursing (1966), university college (1968),[7] school of law (1976), school of business administration (1970) as the undergraduate school of business, Kodak College (1975), and the most recent school of computer science and information systems (1983).

The school of business administration, whose origin dates to the founding of the university in 1906, offers programs on all campuses of the university and has the largest undergraduate enrollment. Through seven departments, the school offers fifteen major concentrations, as well as a B.B.A./ M.B.A. degree in public accounting in conjunction with the graduate school of business.

The graduate school of business, originally the graduate school, is now, according to an American Assembly for Collegiate Schools of Business (ASCSB) survey, the largest such graduate school by total enrollment in the United States.[8] This school offers on all campuses a DPS (doctor of professional studies in management degree--a program for experienced executives), an executive MBA (degree program for managers), master of business administration, and master of science degrees. As an indication of the school's innovative programming, mutually sponsored coordinate degree programs have been developed with other universities, the result of inter-institutional cooperation (e.g., a Ph.D. degree in applied economics with a state university), as well as joint degrees initiated with other schools of the university itself (e.g., J.D./M.B.A. with its school of law).

Successful on-site programs are offered in many neighboring corporations during working hours to meet management development needs. Additional degree programs are constantly being planned (e.g., a proposal for a Ph.D. program in business administration to start in 1988). Another example of entrepreneurial programming is a master of business administration degree for managers from Brazil which has been offered since 1982.

The college of arts and sciences offers a Psy.D. (doctor of psychology in school/community psychology) to prepare professionals for work in schools and the community, master of science, MS/Ed. (school psychology), master of public administration (one in health care management and one in

Institution III (Chase University)

government), bachelor of arts, bachelor of science, associate in science, associate in arts. Combined B.A./M.B.A and B.S./M.B.A. programs are offered through both schools.

The school of nursing on the Bethlehem campus is a result of arrangements made with two hospitals: the transfer by a suburban hospital of its undergraduate school of nursing to the university and, in 1973 through an affiliation agreement between the university and a medical college, the transfer of a graduate school of nursing to the university on the same Bethlehem campus. The latter affiliation resulted in a sharing of trustees and academic resources, as well as the development of academic programs in the medical sciences. Degrees offered in the programs include MS (generic program) and MS (in seven specialty programs).

The school of education offers an MS in education in administration and supervision, and one in curriculum and instruction. The university's newest school (1983), school of computer science and information systems, offers programs leading to the B.S. and M.S. in computer science, B.B.A. in management information systems, and an M.B.A. in information systems.

The first of the university's multicampuses, Bethlehem, was established in the 1960s when the college expanded to the suburbs of a neighboring county, Fairchild, to which industry and corporations were moving. In 1962, on property which was a gift from an alumnus trustee, a two-year college campus was built which today covers 200 wooded acres. The trustee had also donated his large home and funds to purchase adjacent property to create this campus. The first class was offered in 1963. In 1965 the charter was amended by the regents to authorize the university to offer on that campus baccalaureate degree programs in business and in the liberal arts. From an original student body of 143 full-time and 265 part-time students in 1963, the enrollment today on that campus consists of approximately 5,000 day and evening students.

In 1975 the university moved into its second campus when it consolidated with Kodak College, a former Catholic college that had been established in 1923 for young women; in 1971 the name of the college had been changed and it had become coeducational. The agreement with the university stipulated that Kodak College remain essentially unchanged, a mini-university with several disciplines building upon the foundation of a strong liberal arts college.[9] It remains today Kodak College within the university structure. Some ten miles away from the other suburban campus, this campus on twelve acres in the county seat initially had 675 students. Today the campus offers, in addition to Kodak College, graduate programs in business (in an office building in the downtown section of a business community nearby which is corporate headquarters for many companies), education, computer science and public administration. The campus has 800 undergraduate and 400 graduate students. A school of law opened on that campus in 1976, with a new building completed in 1979.

After conducting a survey of businesses in the metropolitan city of its origin to determine the opportunity for expanding its services, the university established a midtown center in 1976 as an extension of the Dupont campus. The center provides baccalaureate and masters degrees, mainly in business, to people working in the area. More than 2,000 students have enrolled in the succeeding years for early morning (7:00-8:40 A.M.) and evening (6:00-9:00 P.M.) classes. Since this location is only fifteen minutes

Institution III (Chase University)

away by public transportation from the Dupont campus, students are able to utilize the full resources of the university.

The most recent expansion as a multicampus university was the purchase in 1977 of a bankrupt college (Kellog) on fifty acres two miles away from the Bethlehem campus.[10] The university was thus able to resolve its shortage of dormitory space and move the graduate division of the school of nursing there for a period of time. Although courses are no longer taught on that campus, the campuses are now referred to as a combined campus (Bethlehem/Kellog) and administered as one campus, with frequent bus service between the two locations.

Each of the campuses has its own unique mix of students. The greatest number of dormitory residents are at the Bethlehem/Kellog campus, the smallest at Kodak. Kodak campus offsets this with a greater number of commuters than Bethlehem as its emphasis is more upon graduate and professional programs for a commuting population. At the Dupont campus, located for the most part in one building, almost the entire student population consists of commuters.

The median family income of the Dupont campus student is somewhat lower than that of the Fairchild county (Bethlemen and Kodak) student. The average Fairchild county student has a car; the Dupont campus student does not. Twenty-five years ago the Dupont student body was approximately 85% male and 15% female; now enrollment is almost equally divided between the sexes, with about half of the adult female students employed. Until recently the two Fairchild county campuses had a much larger percentage of mature women students than the Dupont campus, in part due to the extensive nursing programs offered at Bethlehem. Determined to attract the non-traditional student to its Dupont campus, the university offers classes from 7 A.M. until midnight; evening part-time students, especially in the Dupont campus, continue to represent a significant portion of the total enrollment.

More international students, many from the West Indies, attend classes on the Dupont campus than on the other campuses. A 1977 article with a profile of the student body stated that approximately 23 percent of the university's full-time students were black or Hispanic, with a higher concentration on the Dupont campus. True of all the campuses was the large percentage of students who were the children of parents who did not graduate from college.[11] The identities of each of the campuses strongly reflect their constituencies and the curricula offered.

Organization and Administration of the University

Reorganization of positions and titles of the administration has occurred frequently in this university. Most recently in August 1984, governance was restructured when the long-term president was appointed chancellor and chief executive officer by the board of trustees in preparation for his retirement; his close associate, who had been president of the board of trustees and a former corporate executive, was appointed fourth president and chief operating officer. The chancellor and chief executive officer was still very much in charge of the university at the time of this study.

In addition, after the death of the university provost, that title as the chief academic officer was eliminated and the extensive academic and academic support responsibilities were divided between an executive

Institution III (Chase University)

vice-president for academic affairs and an executive vice-president for institutional planning, management and support services.[12] The deans of the schools and colleges of the university, the university librarian, the director of cooperative education, and the vice-president for corporate and international programs were made responsible to the executive vice-president for academic affairs.

In April 1985, under yet another reorganization, the position of provost was reinstated and the position of executive vice-president for academic affairs abolished (see figure 11). The university librarian now reports to the provost, as do the academic deans, university director of cooperative education, vice-president of academic development, and the two campus deans of studies.[13] The provost and four executive vice-presidents (university relations, institutional planning and academic support services, finance and administration, Fairchild county), report to the chancellor through the president.[14] Reporting directly to the president are vice-presidents for student services, career planning, Kodak, Bethlehem/Kellog, corporate and international programs, and management and computer information systems.

At the time Kodak College became part of the university, a vice-president and an academic dean were appointed for that campus and for the Bethlehem campus. There were no comparable positions on the Dupont campus as the president's office has been located there and the need for another level of administration was not indicated. The vice-presidents for the individual campuses do not have direct responsibility for academic affairs, but rather deal with the administration of their respective campuses. A system of matrix man-

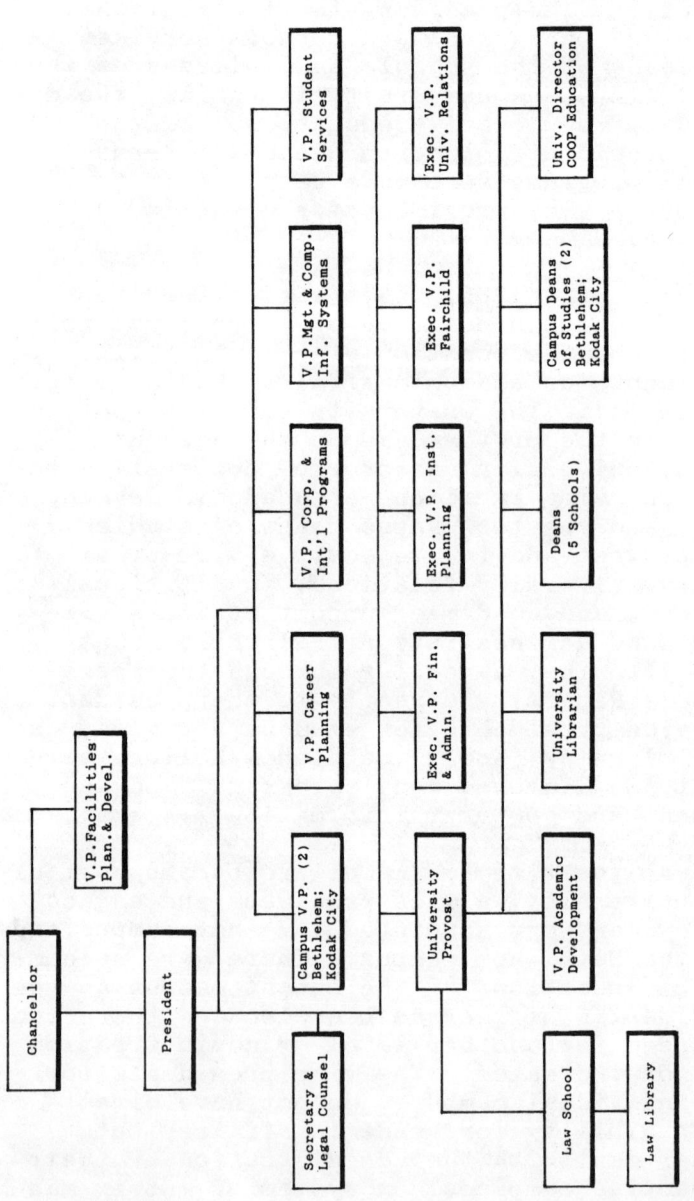

Figure 11
ORGANIZATION CHART: CHASE UNIVERSITY

Institution III (Chase University)

agement is practiced in this university also --a system defined by the vice-president of Kodak as one in which administrators report to more than one person, generally two. Although the two county campuses are very close geographically, they are dissimilar. The multicampus university is described by the vice-president for the Kodak campus as three very different campuses under the same university banner, but reflecting different communities.[15]

The chancellor identified as a major step forward in faculty and university relationships the establishment about twelve years ago of a university senate with representation of faculty, staff, and students.[16] The university senate has provided for faculty councils on each of the campuses for the undergraduate faculty, with a single university-wide faculty council for the graduate faculty. The university is not unionized.[17]

As in most universities, the law school has an existence of its own within the university structure. The autonomy of the law school has been accepted from its beginning; this autonomy was established largely through regulations of the American Bar Association, with the principle accepted de jure but not always honored de facto.[18]

In answer to the question raised by this researcher as to whether the university is an example of a consolidated system with influence evenly distributed among the member campuses or a flagship system with one campus favored over the others, such as a main campus and lesser ones, the answer varied. At Bethlehem the library staff feels that the multicampus university has finally recognized, after a struggle, that it is a consolidated system,[19] even though it is the perception of those at the Dupont campus that they are the lead campus of a flagship system, best characterized as "the first among equals."[20] The chancellor himself continues to view the Dupont campus as the flagship campus, the central and headquarters operation of the university. It is his determination to preserve a strong central structure since, in his view, too many multicampus institutions have suffered from separate campuses succeeding in going their own ways with no centralized structure to restrain them.[21]

However, today the university must be viewed as an example of a consolidated system as the Fairchild county campuses continue to expand in enrollment, construction, and influence. While the Dupont campus is the oldest, and the executive officers are located there, the system allows a fair degree of autonomy among all the campuses. General policy and guidelines are set for the university by the board of trustees, president, and the chancellor; yet within those guidelines freedom exists for the campuses to administer themselves.

The university is approximately 85% tuition dependent,[22] with the remainder of a $100,000,000 university budget derived from endowments, gifts and investments, and income from buildings and university owned bookstores.[23] In addition, state aid contributes $4,000,000. All campuses appear to have equal access to financial resources through policy and organizational structure. Each dean submits a projected budget, with no budget favored over another.

The lack of a significant endowment has formulated the president's operating philosophy. He has said, "Every year is a new year. It is necessary to earn your way, like a business, and you must balance the bottom line. Decisions are tough but possible."[24]

Institution III (Chase University)

The university is bracing itself for the problems of declining enrollment, a condition which many private universities will confront for the next decade, especially in the face of increasing competition from state universities. In 1969 the metropolitan city university's open admission policy had a substantially adverse effect upon Chase University's enrollment. This resulted in several years of operating deficits. The university's leadership has plans to cope with current and future contraction. They intend to run the organization more efficiently and more effectively with fewer employees,[25] and pare the variety of course offerings without hampering the educational program. If faced with retrenchment, the ratio of adjunct faculty to full-time faculty may be increased. Also, the prospect of declining enrollment at one location can partially be offset by shifting faculty to another location,[26] a benefit inherent in a multicampus organization. In addition, with an eye to its market, the university plans to differentiate their product in ways they have not done before.

It is the belief of the executive vice-president for academic affairs (now provost) that the term "contraction" is not acknowledged in the vocabulary of the administration.[27] To the contrary, from 1963, with the gift of property in Bethlehem and the plan to open there a two-year feeder college for the university, the university became a multicampus institution and continued to expand with new campuses and the creation of new space. In 1982 the university launched a $25 million physical development program of new construction: on the Bethlehem campus, a recently constructed library; on the Kodak campus, a new building for graduate studies; and on the Dupont campus, an expansion of the main building by adding three floors.

The university has a reputation for marketing ability. One example: examining the needs in a county notable for its high concentration of scientific and pharmaceutical firms has led the university to offer programs such as a combination business and science degree. Further, with the expansion of the biology and chemistry facilities on the Bethlehem campus, new programs in these business and industrial areas will be offered.

To deal with competition from the metropolitan community college near the Dupont campus, the university is seeking to secure a firm relationship with it so that the community college graduates will transfer to the university for their senior college. The midtown center can be considered a tool for expansion as it continues to attract many students who go on to become students in the Dupont campus.

Description of the Campuses

Dupont Campus

After being housed in a series of rented office buildings in the financial area of the city in its early years, the university purchased and moved to a sixteen-floor building in 1956. Thirteen years later, it built the Dupont campus not far from the original 1906 site, surrounded now by financial, business and governmental institutions. For the most part a self-contained complex with an enrollment of approximately 11,000 undergraduates, it is readily accessible via several types of public transportation. The $17.5 million complex extends over a two-and-a-half acre site, including in addition to classrooms, an eighteen-story tower for offices and dormitories, a science/mathematics center, a computer center, gymnasium, theatre-auditorium, and a library. In 1982 as part of a

Institution III (Chase University)

$25 million physical development program, the university expanded the campus by adding three floors to the tower and completely renovating several of the four nearby buildings also owned by the university. The Dupont campus, then, consists of a skyscraper and subordinate buildings with no grounds.

Bethlehem/Kellog Campus

This beautiful campus actually consists of two campuses two miles apart. Of the two, Bethlehem campus is the center of academic activity. Approximately an hour's drive from the Dupont campus, Bethlehem is situated on approximately 200 acres of rolling rural countryside in one of the country's most affluent counties. Today dormitories house more than 300 students, with additional dormitory provisions at the nearby Kellog campus. Its fourteen buildings, many the result of gifts by alumni and trustees, are eclectic in architecture, ranging from Georgian to contemporary. The most recent addition (1983) is the library building, a winner of a design award, overlooking a pond and dominating the campus. To accommodate the current demand for additional dormitory space on the Bethlehem campus, a project of townhouse dormitory construction is underway.[28]

Ever alert for new sources of revenue, the university had purchased the Kellog campus expecting to use the classroom buildings for additional enrollment. Due to limitations imposed upon parking by the local community, it has become more feasible to keep the campus primarily as dormitory accommodations for university students, utilizing the classroom space as income producers by renting them to large corporations for corporate training using university faculty; this is a separate enterprise and profit center.

Most of the science programs of the two county campuses (chemistry, biology, physics) have been moved to the Bethlehem campus, joining the undergraduate and graduate nursing programs. With the chemistry program seeking accreditation, funds are being directed on the Bethlehem campus to a major renovation of the science and laboratory facilities. The nursing program, which offers seven speciality masters degrees and a generic master's in nursing, has grown to the point where its enrollment represents one-third of the students on campus. In Bethlehem the local ambience and student life are undergraduate and residential.

Kodak Campus

The most recent addition to the university is the Kodak campus created in 1975 by purchasing Kodak College and then building a law school,[29] and in the city of Kodak itself, a graduate center for the graduate school of business. A consultant's report in 1977 recommended that a graduate business school be located in Kodak City because of the city's potential for business and corporate growth. The university is a condominium owner of four floors reserved for the graduate center in a seventeen-story building under construction at the time of the study.

The property of the former Kodak College continues to house the original order of nuns who sold the college to the university and many of the original faculty members who were teaching when the college merged with the university are still on the faculty.[30] On the twelve acres, buildings which have become an integral part of the campus include in addition to the law center (1979)[31] a library building, classroom and dormitory buildings, computer facilities, and administrative offices. To supplement these facilities the

Institution III (Chase University)				177

campus rents additional space in buildings
still owned by the order of nuns.

As a separate and distinct entity with a
liberal arts concentration,[32] Kodak College
can offer its students the resources of the
entire university, including a transportation
system that operates between the two county
campuses every fifteen minutes. Since the
county campuses are no more than ten miles
apart, students at both campuses enroll in
courses at either location, electing specialized courses at either site.

The Kodak campus, separately from Kodak
College housed there, focuses upon graduate
level programs mainly in the graduate school
of business. The campus is virtually the
sole source of education in Fairchild county
for programs in business, computer science,
public administration, and health management.
The development of a graduate degree in international business is in process and the
graduate business school center under construction will emphasize further the graduate
business strength of the campus. The new
graduate school facility ideally situated in
the financial center of the county is expected to attract many students from corporations in the surrounding area. The Kodak
campus, however, has a problem of space due
to increased enrollment.[33] The campus is
landlocked; needs for parking space,
additional classrooms, office space, and residence halls create deterrents to substantially increasing the number of students.

B. THE UNIVERSITY LIBRARIES: STRUCTURES AND
PROCESSES

A mission and goals statement for the
libraries appears in a university proposal
for American Assembly for Collegiate Schools
of Business (AACSB) accreditation:

The University's policy is to provide
library materials in support of the
curriculum on each campus, to develop
specialized research collections as
needed, and to provide professional
assistance for instruction in the use of
the library during most of the hours
that the facilities operate.[34]

The university collection of some
760,000 volumes is distributed among the following units: Dupont campus, serving the university in the metropolitan financial district and in the midtown center: 323,000 volumes; Bethlehem/Kellog: 210,000 volumes; Kodak campus, serving in addition the nearby off-campus location of the graduate business school: 78,000 volumes; and the law school library, also located on the same campus: 150,000 volumes. The growth of the university's libraries reflects the growth of the curricula on each campus. In 1961, the only library of the institution consisted of approximately 46,000 volumes and had an operating budget of $89,500. In 1985 the university libraries had an operating budget of over $2.2 million. The university has built three new libraries on its multicampuses within fifteen years, an indication of the commitment by the university and administration to support the curricula.

Description of the Campus Libraries

Dupont campus Library

The Dupont campus library, established in 1933, has a collection of 323,000 volumes housed on two floors of the busy Dupont campus center serving 19,000 students. The current building was completed in 1969, with the library occupying its quarters in the summer of 1970. Designed to hold 250,000 volumes,

Institution III (Chase University)   179

the library has exceeded that number and "is rapidly approaching capacity in terms of accommodating people, materials, and equipment".[35] In 1984 an additional 10,000 square feet was added at the top of the building, but although some reading space was gained, the library's stack space problems have not been lessened.

The entrance to the library is on the main floor of the building, conveniently located to all students and their activities. As a result of its location and collections, the library is heavily used at all times of the day and evening.

Bethlehem Campus Library

The new library facility which opened in September 1983 to serve 7,000 students is a handsome, functional building, creating a strong presence on the campus because of its central location and striking design. A two-story, $5 million red brick building, named in honor of the chancellor and his wife, it was designed to have space for over 250,000 volumes and has a 600 person seating capacity. While the collection of 210,000 volumes is essentially the same as it was in its previous location as a part of another building on campus, it is now perceived as a greatly improved library by faculty and students who previously criticized its contents.

After the acquisition of Kellog College, the Kellog library was maintained for a time unchanged until the direction of the campus was determined. In June 1982, the Kellog library was closed, and its liberal arts collections were dispersed among the three campus libraries based upon need, with many of the art volumes in particular becoming a source of enrichment to the Bethlehem library collection. The Kellog library had strengths in literature, psychology, and education,

collections which when transferred to the
Bethlehem library were complementary to its
business emphasis. With the merger of the
undergraduate and graduate nursing programs
from Kellog into the Bethlehem campus, the
library collections were merged, too.

The state requires a detailed self-study
incorporating library support whenever registration of a new program is requested. In
preparation for a proposed Ph.D. program in
nursing on the Bethlehem campus, the reader
services librarian has been invited to participate with the nursing department in collection planning, not a usual occurrence.

Kodak Campus Library

The collection of Kodak College library,
the smallest of the three libraries, numbers
approximately 78,000 volumes. Located in a
separate building adjacent to the law school,
it suffers from inadequate stack space and
insufficient reading space. The library had
been built for the Middle States reaccreditation in the 1960s as Kodak College had been
told at an earlier accreditation that the library's original accommodations were inadequate.

At the time of the consolidation with
the university, the library's holdings included a liberal arts collection with particular strengths in history, English, French
and Spanish literature, and the classics;
some had been donations of private collections. Prior to the consolidation, to be eligible for special state aid in the late
1960s, parochial colleges were compelled to
satisfy fourteen criteria, one of which was
the assessment of the library's holdings in
philosophy and theology to assure impartiality in the collection. To prepare for this
special state aid, the library's holdings in
philosophy and theology were enlarged to in-

clude various schools of thought. Thus the breadth of the liberal arts collection was increased further, and has continued to be an important feature of the library's holdings.

A problem for the Kodak campus library is the fact that the graduate business school is not located directly on the campus but in the center of Kodak City. An unknown factor is the kind of library facility planned for the new graduate business center under construction in the city. A reading room has been suggested in the new center with a key collection of important current business literature. University shuttle buses could be made available to transport students from the graduate center to either county campus library.

All members of the university community have complete access to the facilities and resources of all campus libraries, including the law school library. That library is a great asset to many of the business courses, especially in the tax field; tax research courses are scheduled intentionally as close as possible to the law library rather than at the graduate center.

Organization, Governance and Administrative Structure of the Libraries

The single library of the university grew to become a multicampus library system over a span of forty-three years: the Dupont campus library was established in 1933; the Bethlehem campus library in 1963; the Kodak campus library in 1975; the law library, on the Kodak campus, in 1976.

Each campus library is supervised by a library chief who reports to the university librarian. An exception is the law librarian who reports to the dean of the school of law but keeps the university librarian informed. Responsibility for the supervision of the audio-visual departments on the Dupont, Bethlehem and Kodak campuses was transferred to the university librarian effective January 1983. Reporting to him also is the new position of archivist.

The position of university librarian was created in 1980. With his appointment to that position, the new university librarian relinquished his previous responsibility as chief of the Dupont campus library and a new chief was appointed. Previous titles of what was now university librarian included chief librarian in 1961 and director of libraries in 1966. It was with the latter title that he assumed responsibility for the first multicampus library, Bethlehem campus, while continuing to be chief of the Dupont campus library until 1980. A chief of the Bethlehem library was appointed in 1967.

Originally the present university librarian reported directly to the president. As the university grew, the university librarian reported to the provost, as did the academic deans, until that position was eliminated at the death of the provost in 1983. With the reorganization that followed, the university librarian reported to the executive vice-president for academic affairs. Now that the position of provost has been reinstated and assigned to the former vice-president for academic affairs, the university librarian again reports to that position.[36] The university librarian is the only librarian with university-wide authority, and as such participates in decision-making by academic deans and vice-presidents.

As an acknowledgement of the importance of the position and as a tribute to the university librarian, he was honored by the president and the board of trustees in 1982

Institution III (Chase University) 183

with the title of officer of the university.[37] With this title comes the responsibility of assistant secretary of the corporation.[38]

Each campus library exhibits a vertical organizational structure, with the libraries having a combined staff of thirty-one full-time librarians including the campus chiefs and twenty-seven full-time nonprofessional employees. They are distributed as follows: the Bethlehem library (see figure 12) has three department heads: reader services (with responsibility for reference, periodicals, circulation), cataloging, and acquisitions (a total of six professionals and thirteen support staff); the Kodak campus library (see figure 13) has professional positions for business reference, reference and interlibrary loan, cataloging, circulation, evening/weekend, and periodicals (a total of six full-time equivalent professional staff and five support staff); the Dupont campus library (see figure 14), with the largest staff, (twelve professional positions including the chief and thirteen support staff) has a reader services librarian (with responsibility for circulation, interlibrary loan, reference, periodicals librarians), head cataloging librarian (with other cataloging librarians and cataloging assistant positions), acquisitions librarian, and collection maintenance supervisor.

In the law school library (a total of six professionals and six nonprofessionals), two department chairmen report to the law librarian: public services, with responsibility for government documents, reference, and circulation; and technical services, with responsibility for collections maintenance, acquisitions, and cataloging. The law librarian is a member of the professorial staff of the law school. The other professional staff of the law library do not have faculty status

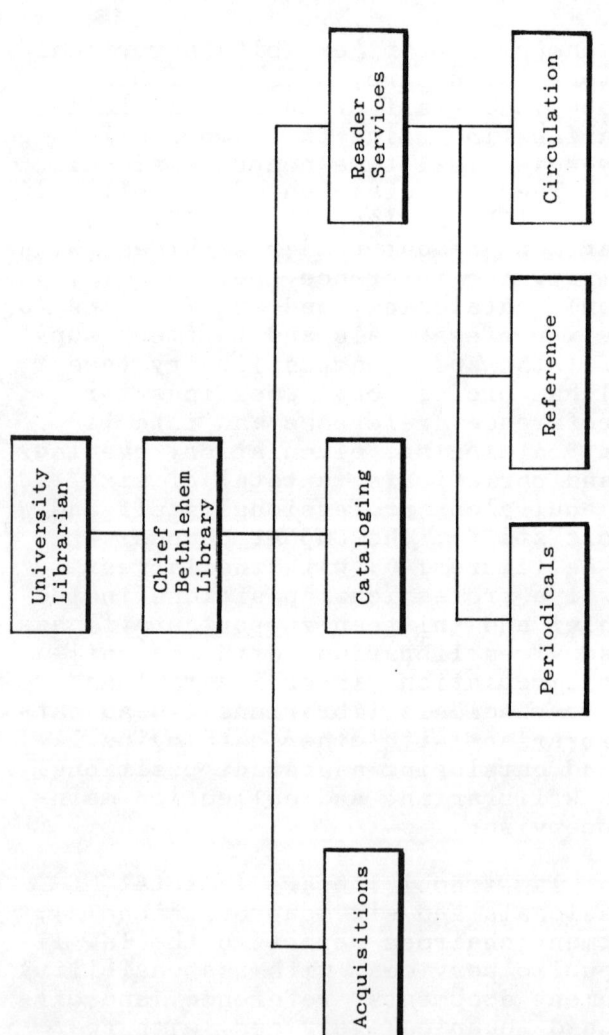

Figure 12
ORGANIZATION CHART: CHASE UNIVERSITY, BETHLEHEM CAMPUS LIBRARY

Institution III (Chase University) 185

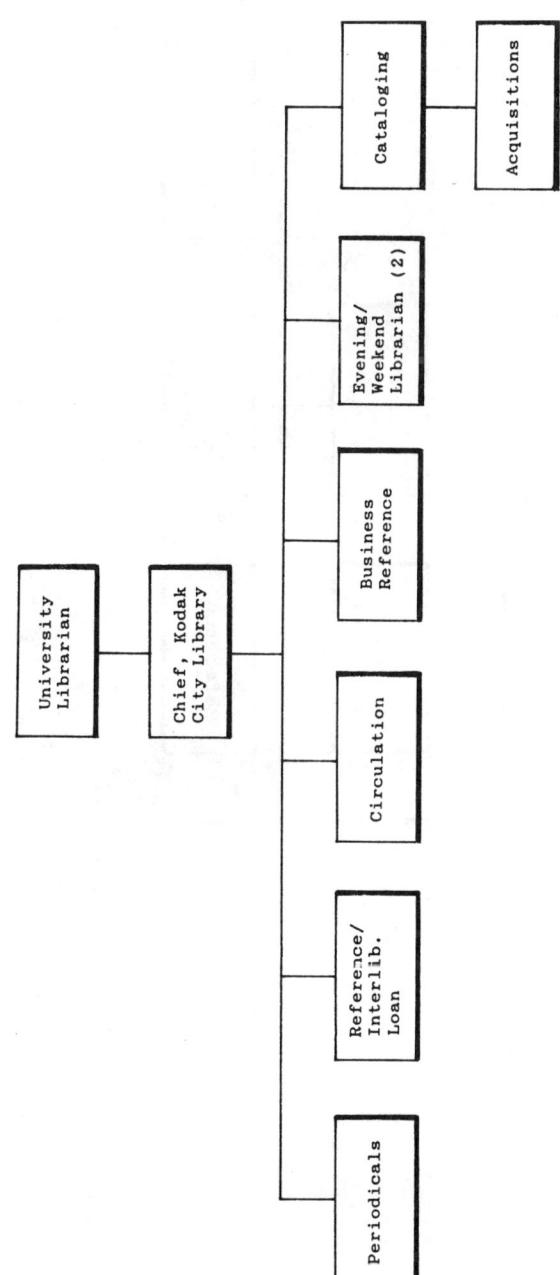

Figure 13
ORGANIZATION CHART: CHASE UNIVERSITY, KODAK CITY CAMPUS LIBRARY

186   Multicampus Libraries

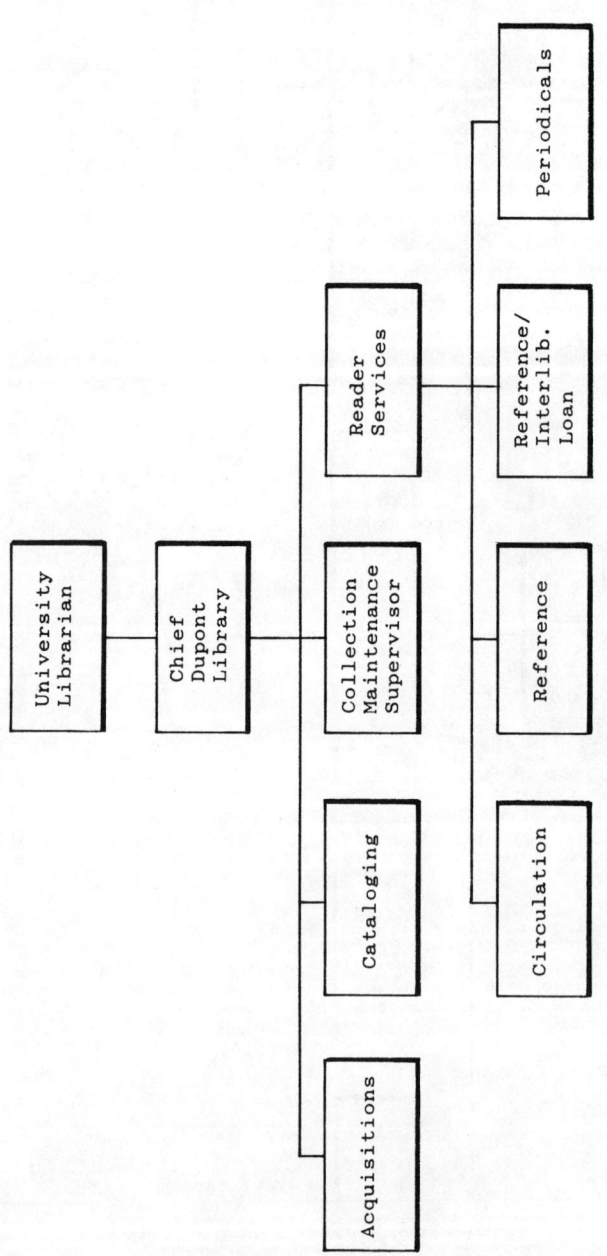

Figure 14
ORGANIZATION CHART: CHASE UNIVERSITY, DUPONT CAMPUS LIBRARY

Institution III (Chase University)   187

and cannot participate in instructional programs since they do not hold law degrees.

Campus library chiefs have responsibility for implementation of university library policies and for day-to-day library operations. Library department heads report to them (there are no assistant library directors). Suggestions are solicited from the department chairmen, and where no such position exists, from the professional staff. In day-to-day operations the library chiefs have local authority, but for long-term planning, centralization of control is in effect. (The balance between centralization and local autonomy has been described as 70%/30%).[39] System-wide policies and budgets for the campus libraries are promulgated by the university librarian, with all campus libraries abiding by university-wide procedures to promote consistency and uniformity.

Little formal written policy exists; policy and operational procedure manuals date back some ten to twenty years and, in the face of new technology, are obsolete. Nevertheless, it is the consensus that library standards and operating procedures are uniform throughout the multicampus system, although local circumstances can modify the uniformity.

The university librarian establishes basic policies after discussion and agreement, usually through the mechanism of the Council of Librarians. A policy making body, the Council of Librarians, composed of the campus library chiefs with the university librarian as the de facto chairman, meets to address and decide system-wide issues. (The law librarian is invited to attend.) Such system-wide matters have included planning for automation, personnel procedures, decisions involving money, and creating and justifying new positions. Final decisions are then made by the university librarian who has complete budgetary control. An example of planning by the Council of Librarians was preparation for online bibliographic searching with ongoing discussions concerning uniform database charges. A present example is the production through OCLC of the union list of serials of the holdings of all the campuses, with input by each campus library.

Personnel matters such as interviewing of staff, staff assignments, duties and responsibilities are decisions made at the campus level. In the case of professional appointments, the campus library chief makes recommendations and confers with the university librarian, who also interviews the applicants. Programs a campus library may want to initiate must be cleared with the university librarian. Requisitions for equipment and specialized library supplies are forwarded directly to the university librarian for approval. Law school library invoices also are sent to him for initialling before being approved by the business office. Each library is responsible for its book selection, with the exception of titles costing over $100, which must be approved by the university librarian. New periodical purchases are also submitted for his approval and signature.

Though library chiefs maintain liaison with each other, in particular the two Fairchild county directors, department heads of the three campus libraries have infrequent contact other than by telephone. Intercampus loans are requested among the campuses, but without an online union catalog, fulfillment is not always successful. With a printed union list of serials, libraries are able to fill journal titles.

Except for the Kodak campus library, faculty library committees exist for all li-

Institution III (Chase University)

braries, including the law school library. However, most committees are inactive. The ten members of the Bethlehem committee, for example, rarely attend committee meetings, although its chairperson is active in such library matters as collection development. At the Dupont campus library, where the university librarian has his office, the faculty council committee meets infrequently and any contact with faculty members by the campus library administration is through the university librarian rather than the chief of the Dupont campus library.

On each Fairchild county campus, a campus dean of studies has been appointed to maintain close liaison between the deans of the schools and colleges and support services and activities such as the library.[40] On the Kodak campus, the dean of studies is also the chairperson of the academic team, a group unique to that campus which functions as a curriculum committee, with a membership of academic chairpersons or assistant chairpersons and administrators. The campus library chief is included in these meetings, thereby alerting the library to new programs, course requirements, and revisions of core curricula. To the chief of the Kodak campus library this is not a reporting relationship, but one whereby, through a professional level of contact, he is kept informed.

The reporting relationship of each campus librarian to the campus administrative officer is termed a matrix relationship by the vice-president for academic affairs, meaning that each campus librarian has, in addition to a reporting relationship with the university librarian, an additional responsibility to the local vice-president of the campus. It is the policy of the university librarian that campus library chiefs as administrators are welcome to attend every meeting of committees or organizations such as the faculty council, but their primary reporting lines are clearly and unequivocally to the university librarian. The vice-president for each county campus has no direct responsibility for campus academic affairs but rather deals with the administration of the campus; his primary interest in the library is not with the collections, but with the facility itself, e.g., space, problems with equipment, hours. It is the understanding of the vice-president of the Kodak campus that academic concerns are addressed at the university level with the university librarian, not at the campus level.[41]

Collection Development

Programs frequently have been developed or abandoned without advance notification of the libraries involved, even though the shifting of programs and degrees from campus to campus has an immediate affect upon the libraries' collections. Now however, as the university prepares for application for American Assembly for Collegiate Schools of Business (AACSB) accreditation for the school of business, the libraries are very much involved. An example of the change in the acquisition pattern of a library resulting from a change in program occurred in the transfer of the school of education to Kodak campus. The level of purchasing in education material was immediately reduced on the Dupont campus and its current journals and backfiles in that discipline were conveyed to Kodak.

As soon as the graduate business department was transferred to Kodak, the acquisitions emphasis of that library changed. With the move away from a liberal arts past, the Kodak library was compelled to acquire materials speedily to support computer science, public administration, and business, as well as education. In preparation for the new graduate center of business, the Kodak library has increased the number of its business management periodical subscriptions to support the curricula, canceling those titles no longer deemed necessary.

The Bethlehem campus is preparing for American Chemical Society accreditation. The library, with the advice of the science faculty, consequently has increased its periodical holdings and purchase of books to support this effort. The forthcoming site visit has resulted also in a decision to consolidate most of the science curricula on that campus and transfer the science periodicals from Kodak to Bethlehem. As emphasis upon research in nursing in Bethlehem has increased in recent years, the library's collection of periodical titles and the depth of the book collection has been affected. (On the Dupont campus, only undergraduate programs in nursing are available.)[42]

Few graduate programs other than the nursing programs are presented on the Bethlehem campus. The majority of business courses offered there are at the undergraduate level; even so, the business collection has been a part of the library's strength since the beginning of the campus.[43] Additionally, close cooperation with the other county campus gives further depth to their resources.

The depth and breadth of business courses have always been strong features of the Dupont campus; the graduate school of business had been centered there since its inception.[44] Some programs--business economics, a masters in banking, and the doctoral program--are currently offered only at the Dupont campus. Programs in international business and international finance are also concentrated on that campus. The Dupont library, with the largest book circulation of the campus libraries, is also the oldest, with the greatest depth of collections.

Priorities for collection development for the campus libraries are established through consultation with the university librarian, with the campus library chiefs now submitting the requirements for new academic programs. Rarely had library resources been considered on any of the campuses in the past when programs were established; as a result financing had seldom been provided for new courses. Nevertheless, the libraries always managed somehow to provide support.

The collections of the law library provide additional resources to the campus libraries. The library supports combined programs such as a new health and law program jointly offered by the law school and the school of nursing as well as supporting the business program in taxation. The law library, in turn, requests from the Dupont campus collection more intercampus loans, particularly in the social sciences, than are requested from the law library.

Reference departments have been developed on each campus, and the resulting duplication of indexes and abstracts is accepted. The viewpoint of the university administration is that each library supports the programs on that campus, with a certain amount of duplication expected as one of the facts of a multicampus system.[45] This may not be cost effective, but as each campus library cannot depend entirely upon intercampus loan, it needs to be reasonably independent.

If a particular item is expensive, only the campus whose program requires it makes the purchase. Consideration is given to sharing resources when purchasing a service that is costly; the director of the Kodak library checks the Bethlehem collection to see if such a projected purchase may instead be available there for student use. Some expen-

Institution III (Chase University)

sive reference sets are purchased for the largest campus library, college catalogs on microfiche for example. The Dupont campus has the most recent set with the superseded set sent to Kodak. Extra indexes to the microfiche brokerage house reports are purchased for the Fairchild county libraries; the students can then request a photocopy of a report from the Dupont campus library. Requests for new journal subscriptions are filled by examination of the union list of periodicals of all campuses as well as through consideration of subject areas supported by each campus.

No formal coordinated collection development policies have been established, although a casual and informal understanding exists among the campus library directors as to what specialized areas each campus library will address. For the most part, selections are made by the librarians, with recommendations by faculty encouraged. To facilitate faculty participation, one of the county campus libraries sends a duplicate copy of Library Journal and Publishers' Weekly to the faculty. It is the policy of the university librarian that all faculty requests for titles should be fulfilled, especially if they are for the reserve collection.

Without written collection development policies, the campus libraries follow informal guidelines for collection development using standard book reviewing media. Choice cards had been submitted to department chairmen in the Fairchild county campuses for distribution among their faculty; the response was too enthusiastic, with the result that the book budget was depleted by December or January. The university librarian now has eliminated this procedure, but has suggested that the Choice cards be used for selection by the library staff.

In making purchasing decisions consideration is given to the types of programs to be served, to programs that have a high priority, and to the differing costs of materials by disciplines. When assessment indicates the need for emphasis in specific subjects such as international business and computer science, federal and state grant money is used, when available, to develop those collections.[46] When particular programs such as Woman's Studies and Black Studies were in demand, the Dupont campus library developed collections to support them. When it became apparent that additional funds would be needed for the new master of public administration program on the Kodak campus, the library chief transferred funds within his budget at the expense of other planned purchases. On the Bethlehem campus the library will concentrate upon the expansion of the curricula in chemistry, computer science and nursing and delivery of health care.

Decisions regarding the purchase of materials and equipment are made by the individual campuses based upon local needs. Rarely is thought given to other campuses. However, at times excess equipment is given to another campus if it can be utilized there. All requests for equipment and supplies must go through the university librarian's office; he, in turn, frequently groups orders to benefit from volume discounts.

Personnel Policies

With the exception of the law librarian, the librarians do not have faculty status or rank, nor does the university librarian. (The university faculty has no union.) The university personnel department in conjunction with the chancellor has established basic personnel policies for all university staff, including all the library staff. A new personnel appraisal and management train-

Institution III (Chase University)

ing plan for all full-time university staff has recently been initiated using an outside consulting firm, with the goal of creating a uniform language of evaluation and criteria to judge and improve job performance of university employees. A parallel goal was to update all job descriptions and classifications to make them applicable for all campuses. A final revision of these job descriptions is in process. The university librarian was a member of the benchmark committee that examined the job descriptions and questionnaires; his own position was not evaluated as he is an officer of the university.[47]

A uniform compensation structure exists. The merit pay system which the university employs is based upon rankings of "unsatisfactory," no raise; "average," 5% raise; "outstanding," 9% raise (these are sample percentages). Each year after the local library chiefs have reviewed their staff, the university librarian consults with the chiefs to consider their decisions and their budget allocation for merit increases. To make the process and qualifications uniform and definitions as objective as possible, the personnel department is presenting seminars for the supervisors.

In the reevaluation of job descriptions and classifications, some library positions were regraded, with the library chiefs of the two Fairchild county campuses lowered one level. At the same time the position of the chief of the Dupont campus library was raised one level as his library is twice as large, has a larger professional staff, a greater scale of activity, and a much larger budget.

The policy of the university to offer growth opportunities by promoting from within encourages the move of a librarian from a position in one library to another within the system. However, the geographical distance between the Dupont campus and the Fairchild county campuses makes such a move between them unlikely, as employees from the county campuses might find the commuting difficult. Employees, however, could move easily between the Fairchild county campuses which are no more than twenty minutes apart; this applies as well to the law school library which has attracted employees from the other county campus libraries.

Library Budget Process

The projected cost of academic support services, in which library costs are included, accounted for 9.3% of the total university budget for 1985. The libraries' share of the total budget, if the law library is included, was 3%. Excluding the law library, the share represented 2.3%.[48]

Each campus has its own budget. The Dupont campus library has been the de facto flagship campus library for many reasons: not only was it at one time the only good library facility among the campuses, but it had more staff. Based upon the number of students enrolled on that campus, and as the university library budget was divided accordingly, that library received approximately 75% of the total library budget. Thus the Dupont campus library prospered. In the last five to six years a more equitable distribution of funds among the libraries has taken place, eliminating previous imbalances.[49]

The process for planning, developing, and administering the annual budget has been the same for many years. At the beginning of the budget year, each library's materials budget is formulated based upon past expenditures and projection of income. In February or March the library chiefs receive, through the university librarian, guidelines from the

Institution III (Chase University) 197

executive vice-president for financial affairs with a budget message from the chancellor outlining the financial status and goals of the university based upon anticipated revenues. Following this, the chiefs submit their requests and justifications for the coming fiscal year for books, equipment and materials within the guidelines established for that year. Requests for additional monies for new programs are made at this time. After he has approved them, the university librarian presents and defends the budgets to the academic vice-president and the vice-president for finance. Budgets are divided into continuing operating costs which are addressed immediately; requests for new personnel and for capital acquisitions are set aside for a supplemental budget if funds are available.

The individual library exercises little direct control over the budget formation but does control its administration. It can only request allocations and then accept what is allocated. Once his budget has been approved, each chief has almost total control, except for single book acquisitions over $100 which must be approved by the university librarian. Library chiefs are accountable for the expenditures of their budgets and for remaining within the limits prescribed; the system does not have the flexibility for appropriated funds to be shifted among the campus libraries to meet changing student demand.

The libraries have received varying increments each year in the materials segment of the budget, but not at a level equal to the rising costs of books and journals. The increases allocated have also not been sufficient to provide additional money required for supporting graduate level collections on the Kodak campus.[50] Because the equipment budgets have not been funded as generously as the materials budgets, the condition of the equipment is criticized by all the libraries.

Cooperation and Resource Sharing

Each campus library is part of an area cooperative, either the Fairchild county library association for the county campus libraries, or a metropolitan cooperative agency for the Dupont campus library. In either instance, the libraries rely more upon the local regional cooperative than upon a sister campus which may be as much as thirty miles or more away. However, reference librarians make intercampus telephone inquiries for recommendations, answers to reference questions, and interlibrary loans, mainly from Fairchild campuses to Dupont.

The Fairchild county library system cooperative is a unique consortium of all public libraries and academic libraries in the county. Currently a union catalog of holdings of all members is on microfiche, with funding for local pick-ups and deliveries. Should the desired item not be available in the region, the request is forwarded to the state interlibrary loan system at no cost. As part of the Fairchild County Union List of Serials project, the university libraries participate in free exchange of journal articles among members. (The university county libraries are net borrowers.)[51] A feature of the Bethlehem and Kodak campus libraries' membership in the Fairchild county library association is the ability of their students to obtain a universal library card for all public libraries in the county. Since a major public library not far from the Kodak campus provides free database searches to the public, students of the university can avail themselves of this service.

While the graduate business center is under construction and alternative library

Institution III (Chase University)   199

arrangements are being considered, several
members of the administration have explored
the feasibility of reimbursing the public library (which is directly across the street
from the new building) for university use.
It is the opinion of the executive vice-
president for finance and administration that
use of the public library should be
encouraged. The vice-president for academic
affairs is exploring the possibility of a
joint venture of public and private
institutions with the public library.[52]

Of the approximately 1500 masters students at the Kodak campus, it is estimated
that a high percentage are professionals
working in the area who have good corporate
libraries available to them and use them. In
return, the Kodak campus library and the
Bethlehem campus library fill whatever interlibrary requests the special libraries require. The numerous corporate libraries in
the area of the Fairchild campuses and in the
financial district surrounding the Dupont
campus make many such requests. Corporate
libraries and law firms compensate, however,
by frequently making gifts of desirable books
to the campus libraries.

Several other regional cooperative library organizations exist in addition to the
Fairchild county library association. An association formed recently includes academic
library directors in the county. A proposal
made within that organization concerns coordination of collections, with each library
subscribing to one national newspaper without
duplicating the others. Another local organization is a subcommittee of the Fairchild
county library association composed of all
academic librarians. On occasion, acquisitions librarians of the Fairchild county library association have met to discuss mutual
problems and share experiences. The university has made a financial arrangement with a

medical college a few miles away from the Bethlehem campus to provide access for students in its nursing program to specialized resources which the campus library cannot adequately supply.[53]

Meetings of campus staff with like-functioning staff in other campuses have occasionally taken place. This has not occurred more often probably because of the hour's trip between some campuses. However, the reference librarians are in frequent contact by phone to discuss mutual problems or request assistance. Intercampus bus service is available to transport library materials to any of the campuses, or for students who wish to go to the other campuses to obtain materials.

The law school library, as the only U.S. government documents depository in the university, encourages students and faculty of the university to utilize their facility. The reference librarians of the two county campus libraries refer students to the law collection as needed. The law librarian has arranged for the transfer of certain government documents from the law library's collection to the Kodak campus library (e.g., census publications and Department of Commerce materials) for use by business students and faculty.

Technical Services and Automation

All campus libraries have been members of OCLC since 1978 and do their own acquisitions and cataloging using that utility; technical services operations are fairly consistent and generally uniform. The university librarian indicated that centralizing technical services has never been considered for the multicampus libraries because no library has sufficient space for those procedures, and, in addition, each campus library chief would be dismayed to have that service withdrawn.[54] Currently two of the libraries are engaged in retrospective conversion from Dewey to Library of Congress classification system in preparation for having all their records in machine readable form; the Kodak library has completed its retrospective conversion. An automation consultant brought in by the university recommended the purchase of three OCLC M300 workstations to be installed in the libraries (two in Dupont campus and one in Bethlehem) to accelerate the process of building up the university database.

All campus libraries subscribe to online bibliographic searching services. Through the Council of Librarians, uniform policies pertaining to online bibliographic searching charges have been established; this is one of the university libraries' examples of coordinated planning and implementation.

The Council of Librarians will proceed with planning for an automated system when the retrospective conversion has been completed, assuming the financial realities of the university permit. The Council of Librarians has recently created a library automation committee to prepare for the future selection of a system and to forestall any imposition of automation from the university administration without library involvement.[55] The same library chiefs would like to establish committees to plan for all new technologies.

Summary

Chase University with a total enrollment of approximately 20,000 students and a faculty of 1,600 on three campuses is the second largest independent university in the state. The origin of the university dates to the early 1900s when as a proprietary institute owned by two brothers, courses in professional accountancy were offered in the evenings. From the eponymous founders evolved the current university, from 1935 a non-profit institution which became a college and then in 1973 a university offering diversified undergraduate and graduate programs.

In the 1960s the first of the multicampuses was added, followed by the purchase in the 1970s of an existing parochial college. The major attraction of the university remains today the variety of business programs offered through the graduate school of business (fifteen major concentrations in MBA degrees) and the range of undergraduate business courses in the school of business administration. A total of eight schools are organized under a system of university deans.

It has been expressed that the secret of the university's success is its innovation in programming.[56] The law librarian indicated that the university tends to develop a module, and then proceed to the next module. (The current showcase is the major effort by the university to achieve AACSB accreditation.)[57] The libraries of each campus involved in new programs or new modules have been affected, even if after the fact. The planning of the institution has benefited from serendipitous timing. By expanding programs of service to corporations when they did, some on-campus and some off-campus, the institution has supplemented its income.[58] Planning by the university has deliberately excluded capital intensive programs. (An exception is the new school of computer science and information systems, but the cost of equipment is coming down.) Instead, the university has concentrated its investments in buildings and people, and in libraries.[59]

The university functions as a consolidated system today; while the original urban campus is still the center of administration and influence, the system allows a fair degree of autonomy among all campuses. The organizational structure consists of one chancellor, one president, one executive-vice president for academic affairs (now provost), one dean of each school (whether a single campus or multicampus school).

A university librarian is based on the Dupont campus. Reporting to him are the chiefs of each of the campus libraries (including the Dupont campus library). Within the three campus libraries, department heads report to the chief of each library, the number of department heads and their responsibilities and titles vary according to the needs of the individual library. As do the academic deans, the university librarian reports to the provost of the university.

The campus library chiefs have responsibility for implementation of university library policies and for day-to-day library operations. Policies and budgets for the campus libraries are promulgated by the university librarian, with all campus libraries abiding by university-wide procedures to promote consistency and uniformity as much as possible. A Council of Librarians composed of the chiefs of the campus libraries, the university librarian, and the law librarian meets several times a year to discuss issues relevant to all the libraries. The university has not centralized technical services as no campus library has sufficient space for those procedures and, in addition, each library chief would be opposed to giving up those activities.

Space problems exist in two of the three campus libraries. (The third, Bethlehem, has a new library building.) The Kodak library building requires either renovation or expansion to be in a position to provide quality services as the graduate programs expand on that campus. The university has engaged an architect to make recommendations concerning the space problems of that campus, including those of the library.

The Kodak campus library faces, in addition, a logistical problem, that of providing services to graduate business students who are located in a classroom facility some distance away in the center of the city. This dilemma is compounded by the minimal parking accommodations available to faculty and students at the Kodak campus, with the result that fewer graduate students come to the campus library. It is assumed they are using the public library located near the classroom building. Interim solutions have been suggested: bringing bibliographic instruction to the classroom, the feasibility of a reading room with reserve materials and current subscriptions in the new building or shuttle services to the Kodak campus or even Bethlehem campus, and courier service between the library and the new classroom building. (An eventual online catalog is expected by faculty and administration to be a partial solution.)

The Dupont campus library has for some time lived with a severe space shortage; it is trying to cope with its overcrowded facility by weeding its collections. When the library was built, the original plan had been to expand the facility eventually to the floor above, but the current shortage of classroom space obviates that possibility. As the largest enrollment is found on the Dupont campus, it is a very busy facility with a corresponding need for additional public service staff, bringing a further demand for space. In addition, planning for the library had not anticipated that the university would grant doctoral degrees. Such degree granting means a commitment to at least a

Institution III (Chase University)   205

limited research collection; yet the physical
facilities can not expand to accommodate
this.

The campus library chiefs hope that the
Council of Librarians will provide a significant forum for their viewpoints and recommendations on automation. The increased role of
technology and automation will result in fundamental changes that will have an effect
upon many diverse areas of library management
and organization. The need for additional
space may be ameliorated by technology; space
savings such as realized from microforms
would be an obvious example. Resource sharing will increase with computerization as the
degree of greater access each library can enjoy with an online catalog becomes evident.

The focus of the libraries will change
as the curricula become more specialized on
the individual campuses. The collection in
the Kodak campus library anticipates being
directed extensively to the graduate school,
with emphasis upon business, computer science, and the other graduate offerings. Only
minimum undergraduate support will continue
to be provided for liberal arts but because
of the proximity of the two county libraries
and the excellent collection that exists in
Bethlehem, undergraduate needs will continue
to be met. With the move of the science programs to Bethlehem and the transfer of the
more sophisticated and expensive science
journals from Kodak, the Bethlehem library
expects to develop greater strength in the
sciences.

The geographical separation of campuses
reinforces a tendency on the part of campus
libraries to be self-contained. When one
campus library (Dupont) is an hour's drive
from another, few students will leave the
first to travel to the other. Consequently,
each library will attempt to serve fully its

own particular public. To do so properly means duplicating expensive indexes and abstracts and other costly materials in a period of fiscal restraint. In contrast, when campuses are no more than twenty minutes drive from each other, decisions concerning duplication can be made cooperatively. When the graduate programs in business were shifted to the Kodak campus from the Bethlehem campus, the collection in Kodak was not at that time able to support the program. Therefore, other means of providing resources had to be explored: shuttle service, union catalog, and additional cooperative sharing of collections.

The reputation of the university as a school of accountancy and business is part of its strength [60] and part of its weakness. The need to maintain the ascendency of the business programs has mitigated the commitment to a broader collection development policy appropriate for a true university library. Meeting the needs of business programs comes sometimes at the expense of other programs.

An evolutionary change may be underway. While the university continues to have the largest graduate school of business in the United States, Chase is responding to different types of students, offering them a spectrum of liberal arts programs.[61] As the Dupont campus library is still perceived by some outside the university as a business library only and not a broad-based university library, steps to overcome this perception are being taken by the university and the university librarian.

The history of the university is unique in that one strong man has been president during its growth from an institute to a college to a university and then to a multicampus university;[62] and that one librarian has

Institution III (Chase University) 207

been responsible for the growth of the library into a multicampus library system as the university grew. The mutual respect and confidence they have for each other has created an unusual working relationship.[63] When the university librarian came to the university, there was one small library in one building. During the tenure of both the chancellor and university librarian, they built a campus and a library in the financial section of the city; they built a campus of 200 acres and 4500 students with a handsome new library at Bethlehem; they acquired Kodak College and there developed a graduate curricula and supporting library services, in addition to a law school and law library; purchased Kellog to increase the space for Bethlehem and absorbed a good liberal arts library collection in the process. Building the libraries for these campuses is an achievement of no small order. This could not have been accomplished were it not for the early conviction of the president that a library with standards is important to an institution with standards. The chancellor has stated that a major problem has been keeping the development of the library system in pace with the development of the university, as it is impossible to build a university without a library. Adhering to this policy has meant building libraries and classrsooms while deferring needed athletic facilities.[64]

Kodak College library was a long established library with its own character and identity before its integration into the university.[65] As the religious influence has faded and as changes in curricula have occurred, the campus has adopted more of a university personality, yet there still are vestiges of its life as an independent institution.[66] Kodak campus and the Kellog campus existed as college campuses before being absorbed by the university, while the Bethlehem campus was created as a totally new campus with a new library collection. As a result, the Bethlehem faculty has early on been drawn into the affairs of the emerging library, participating actively in library committees, advising on access and hours, and making recommendations for collections. Together the faculty and the library have grown.

As for the growth of the library system, the chancellor recalled that the original founder of the institute, a bibliophile himself, had created an environment which made it possible to support a vigorous library development. That founder wrote well, lectured brilliantly, and laid a foundation for the library as the intellectual source of support for the efforts of the faculty.[6,7] The essence of the history of this institution is the everpresent fact that so much of it revolves around one person, the current chancellor. The problem the university faces is how to transfer leadership with continuity. While the current administration with the new position of chancellor and the former president of the board of trustees as president is only transitional, the man who joined the institution in 1947, became president in 1961, and chancellor in 1984, is still very much in charge. However, it is anticipated that in the near term the university will be a different institution as the present administration will pass from the scene; the chancellor, president, university librarian, and others who have been with the university since its inception will retire in the next five years.

Notes

[1] Under the terms of its charter, the university is authorized to have a maximum of thirty-nine trustees. "Report Presented for Consideration of the Commission on Institutions of Higher Education Middle States Asso-

ciation of Colleges and Secondary Schools by [Chase] University," March 15, 1977. (Typewritten), p. 20.

[2] [Chase] University Today, Special Issue [Chase]: A Magazine for the [Chase] University Community, 1983, p. 5.

[3] Progress Through People, [Chase] University Chancellor's Report, 1984. p. 36.

[4] _____, "[Chase] University, How to Ignore the Steady State," [Magazine] 9(November 1977): 39.

[5] "... the ... brothers started on a shoestring tied to an insurance policy--and four decades later, when the family owners turned in their stock to the board of trustees, this constituted a gift to the college of about $1 million." Ibid., pp. 38-39.

[6] [Chase] University, A Brief History, n.d., p. 5.

[7] University college, first named the division of general studies, later the school of continuing education, was conceived to help students matriculate into the university's regular degree programs, as well as to enable adult students to take individual courses without working toward a degree.
"Prospective on the Eighties: The Long Range Plan of [Chase] University, 1980-1990," July 1, 1980. (Typewritten), p. 74. In 1984 university college was changed to the division of continuing education and evening studies.

[8] AACSB's 1984-85 School Fact Form Survey and Salary Survey identified the 10 member institutions with the largest total business school enrollments for Fall 1984: in "Top 10 Business Schools by Enrollment ... Master's Degree Program (Total - 4,805)," the university ranked first. In the "Top 10 Business

Schools by Enrollment ... Bachelor's Degree Program," the university ranked fourth. (Total - 7,433).

[9] The agreement also mandated the formation of a new board of trustees with representation by the university and Kodak College.

[10] "When [Kellog] closed down ... [Chase] agreed to take over its land and buildings, worth about $12 million, and assume its debts, estimated at $5 to $6 million." "[Chase] University, How to Ignore the Steady State," p. 37.

[11] Ibid., p. 34.

[12] [Chase] University. "To: The Members of the [Chase] Community; From: [the President]; Subject: Administrative Reorganization," March 1, 1984. (Typewritten), p. 1.

[13] The same positions reported to the same man in his former position as executive vice-president for academic affairs.

[14] As an example of the continued control by the previous president after his appointment as chancellor and chief executive officer, all communications concerning structural changes are issued by the chancellor. In his "Message from the Chancellor, Enhancing the Organizational Structure," April 22, 1985, he stated: "The Provost and the three Executive Vice-Presidents will report to me through the President." (Typewritten).

[15] Interview with the vice-president for Kodak, March 15, 1985.

[16] The university librarian serves as the secretary of the senate.

Institution III (Chase University)

[17] According to the president of the university, the union lost twice. Interview with the president, April 4, 1985.

[18] Interview with the law librarian, March 22, 1985.

[19] Interview with the readers services librarian, Bethlehem campus library, March 28, 1985.

[20] Interview with the university librarian, February 20, 1985.

[21] Interview with the chancellor, March 15, 1985.

[22] In 1984 the chancellor's report listed: "Current Fund Revenues - Tuition and Fees 83.4%; Private and Public Gifts and Grants 5.6%; Auxiliary Enterprises 5.4%; Other 5.6%." Progress through People, p. 31.

[23] The chancellor reported that the university has operated with a balanced budget in each of the past six years, a significant achievement for a private university with a relatively modest ($17.3 million) endowment.

[24] Interview with the president, April 4, 1985.

[25] In a March 17, 1986 "Message from the Chancellor," he addresses the problem of "Our Changing Enrollment and Budget Situation," reassuring the personnel of the university that their positions are not in jeopardy as reduction in expenses are planned. (Typewritten).

[26] "Report Presented for Consideration of the Commission on Institutions of Higher Education Middle States Association of Colleges and Secondary Schools by [Chase] University," March 15, 1977. (Typewritten), pp. 94-95.

[27] Interview with the executive-vice president for academic affairs, March 8, 1985.

[28] Should demographics change, the townhouses can be sold as condominiums.

[29] The president of the university had long planned to build a law school, but was unable to find a site. That led to a consolidation whereby the university agreed to purchase a college and assume its debts; not only was that cheaper than buying property, but in addition the university acquired one of the best sites in that area. Interview with the president of Kodak College at the time of the consolidation, April 10, 1985.

[30] The merger agreement stipulated that the entire faculty of Kodak College would be transferred to the university in their tenure slots in accordance with their personnel history in the College.

[31] Accredited by the American Association of Law Schools (AALS) in January, 1982. In 1980 the school had been accredited by the American Bar Association.

[32] The unusual element of the merger between Kodak College and the university was the agreement that Kodak College would retain its identity instead of the larger institution absorbing the smaller. Interview with the vice-president for Kodak (a member of the board of trustees of Kodak College before the merger), March 15, 1985.

[33] The enrollment has grown from the original 800 students at the time of the merger to 2700-2800 students, not counting the graduate school in town.

[34] "Institutional Self-Study for AACSB (American Assembly of Collegiate Schools of Business) Accreditation: Library and Computer

Institution III (Chase University)   213

Resources, Facilities and Services," 1985.
(Typewritten), p. 184.

[35] "Review of Activities, September 1983-
August 1984," [Chase] University Library
[Dupont] Campus, 1983-84 Annual Report.
(Typewritten), p. 1.

[36] "Message from the Chancellor: Enhancing
the Organizational Structure," April 22,
1985. (Typewritten).

[37] "... not only recognizes the importance of
his position, but also ... 22 years of de-
voted service to [Chase] during which time he
has been instrumental in developing a comprehensive collection of 720,000 volumes and
4,400 periodical titles at the four campus
libraries." "Message from the President:
University Librarian Named an Officer of
[Chase]," December 20, 1982. (Typewritten).

[38] As assistant secretary of the corporation
(the university), he is empowered to sign
documents, if necessary.

[39] Interview with the readers services librarian, Bethlehem campus, March 28, 1985.

[40] "Message from the President, A Summer Update," August 27, 1984. (Typewritten), p. 5.
The campus deans of studies report to the
vice-president for academic affairs.

[41] Interview with the vice-president of Kodak
campus, March 15, 1985.

[42] In 1984 two nursing work-study programs
were established on the Dupont campus in affiliation with two medical centers.

[43] The acquisition of the 25,000 volumes from
the Kellog library provided a perfect complement to the Bethlehem library, since Kellog's

book collection in the humanities and the social sciences had been strong.

[44] In preparation for application for AACSB accreditation, all the libraries expended in 1984/85 a good portion of their budgets for business materials (37% in Dupont campus, 40% in Kodak, 30% in Bethlehem.) "Institutional Self-Study for AACSB (American Assembly of Collegiate Schools of Business) Accreditation," pp. 195-196.

[45] Interview with the executive vice-president for academic affairs, March 8, 1985.

[46] A state coordinated collection development grant, for example, is allocated yearly.

[47] Interviews with the university director of personnel services and the compensation manager, April 11, 1985.

[48] Interview with the executive vice-president for finance and administration, April 8, 1985.

[49] Interview with the chief of the Bethlehem campus library, March 1, 1985.

[50] Interview with the chief of the Kodak campus library, March 1, 1985.

[51] Interview with the director of interlibrary loan of the Fairchild county library system, April 4, 1985.

[52] Establishing methods of cooperation and reciprocity with the public library should benefit the public library as well as the university by obviating duplication of expensive business reference services. Interview with the vice-president for academic affairs, March 8, 1985. Interview with the executive vice-president for finance and administration, April 8, 1985.

Institution III (Chase University)   215

[53] This arrangement was part of the contract at the time the university inherited a generic masters program from the hospital when the hospital was in debt.

[54] Interview with the university librarian, February 20, 1985.

[55] Interview with the law librarian, March 22, 1985.

[56] Interview with the associate dean for faculty and academic affairs in Fairchild county, March 15, 1985.

[57] The law school is no longer the showcase. Interview with the law librarian, March 22, 1985.

[58] The chancellor stated his philosophy: "flexibility to take advantage of opportunity without impeding the development of the academic integrity of the institution." Interview with the chancellor of the university, March 15, 1985.

[59] Interview with the vice-president for academic affairs, March 8, 1985.

[60] As the associate dean of the college of business said: "Our roots are in accounting and business; we have built the university on that." Interview, March 15, 1985.

[61] Applications are under way for the establishment of a Phi Beta Kappa chapter at the university as well as AACSB (American Assembly of Collegiate Schools of Business) accredition.

[62] As expressed by the vice-president for the Kodak campus: "The university for the longest time has been the president (now chancellor) --his personality, his drive, his vigor, his imagination. When that personality leaves,

there is going to be some trauma." Interview, March 15, 1985.

[63] The chancellor stated that the university librarian is a magnificant manager and that the two have worked together effectively long enough to have had an impact upon each other. Interview with the chancellor of the university, March 15, 1985.

[64] Interview with the president of the university, April 4, 1985.

[65] The library of Kodak College had started in 1923 in a convent building, then moved to an administration building, and then to its present library building, all before the college merged with the university. This has resulted in a liberal arts collection which is older than the university's. Interview with the dean of studies and chair, academic team, Kodak campus, March 22, 1985.

[66] Original faculty and building architecture reflect this origin.

[67] Interview with the chancellor of the university, March 15, 1985.

CHAPTER V

SUMMARY AND CONCLUSIONS

Summary

Three multicampus universities, two private and one state-related, located in two states in the Northeast were selected for this study. Their identities have been disguised to preserve their anonymity; pseudonyms have been used for the institutions, campuses and geographic locations. The following aspects of each institution and its libraries were examined using the model developed by Lee and Bowen: (A) the environment in which each library system functions--a profile of the parent university including background and history, student population, organization and administration of the university, the university budget, and description of the campuses; and (B) the library system itself, including organization and administration of the libraries; descriptions of the campus libraries; and processes comprising collection development, personnel policies, library budget process, coordination and resource sharing, and technical services and automation. Lee and Bowen emphasize in their research three themes of origin, organization, and size; these have been addressed in the three institutions of this study of multicampus university libraries.

Through extensive personal interviews with campus and institutional personnel and with library staff, a total of eighty-three interviews were conducted in fifteen locations among the three multicampus institutions that were visited. The three multicampus library systems studied had from approximately 750,000 to 1,850,000 volumes in their collections. The number of professional staff members ranged from thirty-five to seventy. The enrollments of the institutions they served varied from 19,000 to 31,000 full-time and part-time students. Campuses spanned a range of physical size and student density from Institution I (Harrison University) where the flagship campus is many times the size and enrollment of the other campuses and dominates the system to Institution III (Chase University) in which its three campuses are more equivalent in size and have similar enrollment. Institution I is the only one of the universities which was founded in the nineteenth century; its original campus is the flagship campus. The other two institutions can be termed consolidated systems, using the Lee and Bowen typology implying that each system is basically free from the dominance of a single campus.

While all three institutions visibly responded to the demographic changes that occurred in the last thirty years, there is a striking difference in the actions of Institution I (Harrison University) and Institutions II and III (Clemens University and Chase University). Harrison University, the traditional liberal arts institution, adapted to changes in the city of its origin by digging in its heels, dedicating its resources to the inner city and making its campus the main campus and its library the main library while establishing a satellite branch in the nearby business heart of the city. Its acknowledgement of the exodus to suburbia by establishing two outlying campuses is almost token.

Summary and Conclusions

Institution II (Clemens University), which began in a city as a liberal arts school for students of low income who could not go elsewhere, turned its energies from its campus in the decaying city to new campuses in the growing suburbs, attracting middle income students with a wide range of innovative programs. Emerson campus, the first of their suburban campuses, thrived greatly, enjoying as a result the largest campus library in the university.

Institution III (Chase University), a strongly entrepreneurial institution, also expanded aggressively, creating campuses of opportunity in the suburbs to which college-directed populations and corporate businesses fled. However, always noted for its business orientation, it maintained and strengthened its original campus in the heart of a large city's financial center. That is where the university's largest library and the university librarian are located.

Thus, the original urban campus in two of the institutions has undergone a change in role or in mission. In Harrison University a commitment was made by the university not only to maintain the urban campus in its location in a depressed community but to go beyond and consolidate it as the main and pivotal campus. Of the urban campuses of the three universities, this campus is by far the largest in area and in student body. It is not only the flagship campus now but a campus actively involved with its surrounding urban problems. In Clemens University the financial difficulties of the original urban campus have not been overcome, and the first of Clemens University's suburban campuses has become, by default, the main campus while the urban campus continues to struggle to survive. At Chase University the urban campus is one of three campuses and as the oldest has continued to be more important and have greater influence than the largest of its two suburban campuses, in part due to its desirable position in the heart of a city's thriving financial district.

The pattern of expansion was similar among the universities. Each institution had its beginning in an urban setting; the new campuses that were added after World War II were located in suburban areas as the universities, wanting and needing to increase enrollment, followed the migration of people and industry out of the cities. (Harrison University added its first multicampus between the two World Wars--an art school with a narrow academic concentration.) Expansion was through the purchase or lease of preexisting campuses and the creation of entirely new ones. From the late 1930s into the early 1980s, each of the institutions acquired a major estate in an affluent suburban area as the site for a campus, and two of the institutions (Harrison and Chase) purchased an existing college to merge with the main institution. Clemens and Chase purchased or leased one or more church-related colleges to form additional campuses. Extensive growth in student population occurred at all of the newer campuses.

Two of the universities (Harrison and Chase) have created a campus in the center of a metropolitan city to provide courses and programs for people who work in or travel to that part of the city. Off-campus sites have been developed by Clemens and Chase as a source of revenue from new enrollment, in effect increasing their university's markets. In addition, Clemens University made a formal agreement with an undergraduate college to offer graduate courses on that site, sharing expenses and dividing profits. Clemens University has further explored the market potential for new students by expanding its multicampus operations within geographical

Summary and Conclusions 221

boundaries greater than the other two universities.

The effect of geographic separation of campuses within each institution depends upon two factors: the actual distances between the campuses and the location of the central administration. The central administration of two of the universities (Harrison and Chase) is located on the main campus and at Clemens University on the administration's campus adjacent to the largest and most successful campus. All of the campuses at Harrison University are within little more than half an hour of each other, whether by intercampus bus or by public or private transportation. Its flagship campus is thereby accessible for use of any of its major facilities, including the library, and for cross-campus registration. The location of the central administration on that campus adds to its importance. The six campuses of Clemens University are widely dispersed, with distances requiring one-and-a-half to two-hour trips from some campuses to others. The fact that the central administration is located not far from the most successful campus, its suburban campus, ties those two together in the university. While two of the campuses of Chase University are only twenty minutes apart from each other, each is over an hour away from the original urban campus. Although central administration is located on the urban campus, the president, chancellor, and other administrators maintain additional offices at the two suburban campuses.

All of the institutions offer a variety of undergraduate and graduate programs and degrees, with certain campuses noted for their particular strengths. All institutions have a large business major enrollment and MBA student population. Graduate courses and programs, for the most part at the master's level, are offered on all the campuses of

each university. Each institution offers at
least one Ph.D. program. Among the separate
professional schools, in addition to the MBA
programs in all three universities, are a law
school in one university, medical, dental,
and law schools at another, and a school of
pharmacy in two.

The three institutions have in common a
frequently changing administrative structure.
The restructuring each university has undergone, at times the result of recommendations
by consultants and Middle States accreditation teams, has resulted in varying degrees
of centralization and decentralization
through the years. Clemens University is the
only university of the three to have developed, almost from the beginning of its multicampus existence, a federated system in which
campuses functioned autonomously, each campus
having little in common with the others and
historically manifesting resentment toward
them. Currently, the institution, as a
result of a critical 1982 report, is in the
process of changing from a federated system
to a unified and consolidated organization
via the creation of university faculties cut-
ting across all campuses. The degree of campus autonomy at the other two universities
has also varied. At Harrison University autonomy of the individual campuses is today
minimal as the president and administration
are committed to the strong flagship concept
of the large main campus (which has two-
thirds of the entire student enrollment). At
Chase University the strong personalities and
firm leadership of the long-time president
(currently chancellor) and the university librarian, both in office for over twenty
years, has minimized campus autonomy.

Each university now has a president as
the chief executive officer in whom formally
lies the decision-making power.[1] In practice,
however, actual power in the case of Chase

Summary and Conclusions

University lies with the chancellor, formerly the president; the current president exercises secondary power. (The three institutions all have new presidents, Harrison in 1982, Clemens in 1985, Chase in 1984.)

Each institution is continually revising organization charts to reflect the actual or desirable administrative structure and the reorganization of positions and titles of administration. The charts present a conventional pyramidal command structure. The title of the chief academic officer in each university has varied from provost to vice-president of academic affairs. The individual campus administrative officer bears a different title in each institution: Harrison - dean; Clemens - provost (senior vice-president/university provost of the two largest campuses); Chase - vice-president and dean of the two campuses other than the main campus.

The institutions have experienced both expansion and contraction within the university as a whole and separately on individual campuses. In addition to expansion to new campuses, considerable construction of new buildings and additions to older ones have taken place during the last twenty to twenty-five years in each university. The universities have also undergone periods of declining enrollment, although at different times: Harrison in the late 1970s, Clemens and Chase in the early to mid-1980s. Enrollment problems, however, did not strike at all campuses of the same institution. At Clemens University, they were confined, for the most part, to the original urban campus which never recovered from its location in a neglected neighborhood and from competition of the low tuition of the local city university system. Low tuition at the local public university has had its effect upon Chase University as well.

Each of the universities has a large minority and foreign student population on its urban campus, with at least one campus within the institution educating a large number of first-generation students. In addition, each institution has a suburban student population, largely commuting, particularly in the evening.

All of the institutions examined are tuition-dependent; the two private universities (Clemens and Chase) are approximately 85% so, and handicapped by small endowments. State and federal aid to private institutions has provided considerable assistance to both Clemens and Chase. Harrison University, as a state-related university, receives state support for approximately one-third of its annual budget; it is tuition-dependent for much of the balance. With the absence of sizeable endowments in the three institutions the financial success or failure of an individual campus enrollment has a profound impact upon the overall university budget.

Within two of the university library systems examined (Harrison and Clemens), the striking constant is the changing nature of its administrative structure mirroring the parent university structure, the one changing as frequently as the other. Today each of the library systems seems to be entering into a period of centralization and consolidation as the universities, motivated by the need to be more efficient economically, adjust to a decline in enrollment growth.

While none of the multicampus library systems had assistant or associate directors at the time of the study, Harrison University has had two such traditional positions, assistant director of public services and assistant director of technical services. The fact that the Harrison University library system has had five library directors in ten

Summary and Conclusions

years indicates the many changes that have taken place in the system. The current library director (as of April 1985) has approval to create two associate library director positions again. Until that time, all chiefs of campus libraries and department heads report to the director of libraries (who is also the director of the main campus library).

Clemens University functioned with chiefs of only the individual campus libraries until the new president appointed a university director of libraries in July 1985 to create a university library system--a priority step taken immediately upon his arrival. Within the next budget year, an additional position of assistant director of libraries has been promised to the new unversity director of libraries. Until that time all department heads in the Emerson campus library and the chiefs of all campus libraries report directly to him.

Chase University has a university librarian who has served in that capacity since 1980 but had been with the university as director of libraries with responsibility for one library for approximately twenty preceding years. Each of its three campus libraries has a chief librarian. No assistant director positions exist as the university librarian maintains that the staff of each campus library is too small to require one.

The university librarians in each institution report to the chief academic officer of the university, no matter what the current title of that position might be. In each of the institutions studied some ambiguity has been cited concerning the reporting lines of the campus library chiefs to the university librarian and to the local campus authority due to their form of matrix management. However, little conflict appears on the surface

in any institution. It is clearly perceived
that the primary obligation of the campus library chief is to the university librarian
for library concerns such as collection, administration, budget, while library hours,
space, etc., are considered campus matters to
be discussed with the campus administrator.
In all institutions diplomacy appears to be
practiced to avoid conflict between central
and local authority.

Communication and interrelationships
among the professional staff of the campuses
in a library system depend to a large extent
upon geographic distances, historical relationships, and the policy of the director of
libraries. In Harrison University, the campuses are not far apart; professional meetings encouraged by the new director of libraries take place bi-weekly through an Administrative Council. In Clemens University,
due to the geographic distances between campuses and to their historical autonomy, professional staff not only rarely meet their
counterparts in the other campus libraries
but have infrequent telephone contact with
them. At Chase University, partially due to
the transportation problem, professional librarians have only telephone contact with
each other; campus library chiefs do meet at
least once a semester with the university librarian, however.

Contributing to the libraries operating
as a system is the extent to which technical
services are performed centrally (including
ordering, cataloging, processing). At Harrison University, all technical procedures are
performed by the main campus library staff.
At Clemens University, the Emerson campus
has provided these services for several of
its dependent campuses. Now, with the appointment of the university librarian (still
remaining director of the Emerson campus library) plans have been made for the Emerson

Summary and Conclusions

campus to undertake these responsibilities for all the campus libraries in both regions as soon as staff and funds become available. At Chase University each campus is responsible for its own technical services as no campus library is large enough to undertake the responsibility for the entire library system.

No multicampus library system has produced formal written policy guidelines, with the minor exception of the standardization of circulation policies at Harrison University required by its online circulation system. No multicampus coordinated collection development policies exist in any of the three library systems studied; consideration is given instead to programs that have a high priority, the type of programs served, and the differing costs of materials by disciplines. Several campuses have evolved their own informal collection development policy, in particular the Emerson campus of Clemens University, the only campus in that university with a substantial budget and collection.

For the most part, collection selections are made by the professional staff of each campus library, with faculty participation encouraged; rarely is thought given to other campus collections in the university. The extent of collection development and the staff required for that activity depend upon the size of the library budget. The new director of libraries at Harrison University can now plan for a full-time staff for collection development as the university has increased his budget substantially. This should result in increased intercampus loans throughout the whole system as the collections grow in scope and depth.

Harrison and Clemens have faculty unions to which the librarians belong. Chase has no union and librarians do not have faculty status. Relationships between the chiefs of their campus libraries and the campus academic departments are not affected by this, however. More emphasis is placed on whether the faculty of the campus is a resident faculty and whether there is a campus faculty library committee.

While American Library Association standards have recommended a monetary 5% or higher institutional support of libraries, not one of the three universities studied provided more than 3%. The percentage of the total university budget allocated to campus library budgets ranged from 2.4% (Harrison University last year) to 3% in Clemens University (over 4% for the Emerson campus library budget, balanced by 2.4% for the Thoreau campus library). Harrison and Chase in 1985-86 will receive 3% of the total university's budget. The more customary percentages in the 2.2 - 2.4% level evidence the poor library support previously offered by the Harrison administration. As the budgets of Clemens University are based upon individual campus enrollment, support for campuses not financially successful falls short of anticipated needs; a corollary is that all libraries in that multicampus system are not supported equally. At Harrison and Chase this is not true; all libraries share fairly in the total library appropriation. Campus libraries in each system have control of their budget expenditures, with some imput at the preparation level. However, each must adhere to the final budget. When tuition revenues have been inadequate at any of the three institutions, not only have increases in the budgets not been forthcoming, but cuts have been made. Where increases were feasible, the percentage of increase has been approximately 5% in each institution.

Summary and Conclusions

All university library systems hold memberships in various consortiums, regional cooperatives and networks. In addition to memberships in RLG (Harrison University) and OCLC (Harrison, Clemens, and Chase), campus libraries in each system exchange information and materials more frequently with libraries outside their universities but in their immediate areas, rather than apply to distant campuses in their own institutions. Intercampus exchange of materials is more prevalent within Harrison and Chase Universities, as their main campuses serve as reference and referral points. In Clemens University, until recently a federated system, little intercampus activity takes place between the campuses of the two divided regions. This is due partly to the considerable distance between campuses and partly to the historical division into regions and the resulting psychological separation.

Technology and automation have affected the multicampus institutions to a varying degree. Planning for automation is done centrally at the flagship campus university of Harrison University. Harrison University has an online circulation system in the main campus which is being expanded to the other campuses; plans for a system-wide online catalog and circulation system are underway. Clemens University has an online circulation system operating only for those campus libraries under the aegis of its Emerson campus library; the new university librarian anticipates that this system will be extended to all other campuses. Chase University does not have an online system yet but is completing retrospective conversion of all catalog entries to be ready when a system becomes financially feasible.

Each of the multicampus library systems reflects the history of its university. Harrison University, the oldest of the three institutions, is motivated by its mission to be a people's university. The concentration of efforts to this end may have been a deterrent to the university's hope to achieve important status as a leading research institution. Library resources have had to be applied to meet the needs of its constituent communities at the expense of increasing its collections to that of a comprehensive research library. A recent rededication to the goal of becoming a significant research institution has resulted in a special allocation of $1,000,000 for collection development and library improvements. At the same time Harrison remains principally a commuting university with a student body that contains a high percentage of minority students.

At Clemens University the library of the original urban campus reflects the eclipse of that campus by the newer and more profitable suburban campus. As the urban campus struggles to survive, its library contends with an inadequate materials budget and a reduced staff. In Chase University, a long-time university librarian and a long-time president together created a dynamic multicampus library system from its beginning as a small library in one building. The two strong personalities continue to provide leadership to the university and the library system. When both will retire in a few years, there will inevitably be questions raised about the future direction of the university and the library system.

Conclusions

Three multicampus universities in one geographic region do not constitute a sample of all multicampus university libraries. Yet aspects of governance have been revealed in this research that allow tentative conclusions to be reached which may serve as hypotheses for further study:

Summary and Conclusions

--The distance between campuses bears on the real or desired control which central library administration exercises upon the outlying campus libraries. Greater campus autonomy is bred by greater geographical separation among the campuses, the distance between campuses often dictating communication and strategy of governance. The greater the distance, the more autonomous the local campus library, the weaker the communications and interpersonal relationships with the other campus libraries. It is interesting to see how administrations of the institutions studied have been affected by the distance-between-campuses factor in establishing the type of governance in their universities. Harrison University has been spared the geographical deterrent to centralization, for the greatest distance between campuses is only twenty miles, a matter of approximately forty-five minutes by car. The Wilson campus long has been the main and flagship campus and the Wilson library the largest and strongest.

Clemens University, where campuses are as far apart as one hundred miles, had seemed unconcerned by its lack of operation as a university system and had encouraged a federated governance of free-standing campuses, held together by hardly more than a common name. The inordinate amount of time required to commute between all campuses obviated the possibility of frequent contact by administration, faculty, and students. (It had been suggested, possibly in jest, that the university invest in a helicopter to make intercampus liaison more feasible. The suggestion to date has not been acted upon.)

Chase University, with distances between the furthest campuses not as great as Clemens University, adopted an innovative policy to strengthen intercampus unity and the sense of being an important part of a whole by achieving visibility for its administrators--distances were overcome by establishing offices for the chancellor and president on each campus. The two have made a point of being seen regularly and circulating frequently. Its library director, a strong administrator, likewise keeps in constant contact with all campus libraries.

--The nearness of a campus library to the main campus library inhibits, and sometimes prevents, further growth of the campus library because duplication of collections becomes unnessary or unjustifiable. On the other hand, central library administrations face the dilemma of providing adequate resources to a distant campus library for the latter's programs without extensively duplicating collections. As an example, Harrison University had once been ambivalent about whether to become a suburban institution or remain dedicated to its major urban campus and concentrate the major portion of its energies and resources to that campus. It decided in favor of recommitting itself to its urban beginning, and today, even though the suburban campus (Fillmore) has 60% of the university graduate population of MBA students and a little over 35% of the undergraduate business majors, the current president refuses to consider major growth for that campus. Yet the Fillmore library needs additional space and collections; library reports through the years have reiterated the problem of insufficient volumes for support of on-campus graduate programs. To provide sufficient library support the Fillmore campus library must continue to refer students to the Wilson campus library, knowing it is unrealistic to assume its students will travel willingly and frequently to the Wilson library. Though intercampus shuttle buses and local train service are available, city traffic dictates more tedious and longer trips

Summary and Conclusions

than mileage alone would indicate. The Fillmore campus library of Harrison has been developed more as a satellite to the Wilson campus library than as a support center for the programs offered on its campus. It would appear that this is a disservice to the students of that campus. However, for accreditation purposes, Wilson campus collections are part of the university and considered available.

--The existence of resident faculties and a resident student body on a campus can influence the size and operation of the library on a campus. Harrison University's Jackson campus has neither resident faculty nor resident student body and thus electronic access to the Wilson library can be adopted with duplication of collections avoided. Fillmore campus of that university has a resident student body but no resident faculty; therefore, the faculty evince little interest in the library and its lack of substantial resources. Without strong faculty involvement it is difficult for the Fillmore campus library to make its needs accepted by the administration.

At Clemens University, of the three campuses with no resident faculty or resident students, one campus has access to the library of a campus associated with the university, the other two rely upon other libraries for their academic support (Hawthorne upon Emerson and Dickinson upon a college in the area). Since the student body of its Thoreau campus is primarily a commuting body, the reduced library hours are adequate, whereas the large resident student body of Emerson campus necessitates extensive library hours. At Chase University each campus has a resident faculty and student body; each campus library has been developed to support fully the campus programs and with library hours to support the campus.

--Multicampus libraries seem to operate in a state of frequent change, not always but often the direct consequence of change in university administration. (One library system has had five library directors in ten years.) In this examination of multicampus library systems at a single moment in time, even as the study was under way changes were occurring in each institution. Changes may be schematic or only titular and advancing or receding from centralization or autonomy.

It would appear that administrations of multicampus universities undergo frequent restructuring in a continuing attempt to find the most viable form of administering the campuses. Clemens University is experiencing the most radical change, moving from a federated system where each campus (and its library) was almost completely autonomous to the present unified structure with central authority. A history of frequent changes in administration, responsibilities of positions, and titles may be the reason for today's confusion as to actual authority, reporting lines and the extent of decision-making power of the individual campus. Conflict of authority between the major campus vice-president/university provosts and the university academic deans has surfaced. With the creation of the new position of vice-president of academic affairs this conflict should be ameliorated. In the same institution library reorganization is underway with the creation of a new position of university director of libraries.

As an additional example, at Chase University the changing titles of university administrators have resulted in the frequent issuance of new organization charts as attempts are undertaken to make university governance leaner and more efficient. Frequent restructuring of positions and lines of

Summary and Conclusions

reporting have taken place within recent years at Harrison University and its libraries as well. It appears that constant restructuring of a university and its libraries depends upon the environment at that moment as solutions are sought for administering large organizations with disparate campuses.

--Frequently the creation of a campus and its library has been the action of entrepreneurism and expedience with no allowance for proper planning for facilities or adequate support for the programs. The multicampus developed rarely because such geographical delivery of education was more efficient but more often as a reaction to customer demand. Universities, in effect, were driven by the forces of the marketplace. From the study of three undertaken here one may postulate that institutions that are predominantly tuition-dependent and non-endowed become market-driven and develop an ability to recognize and quickly respond to changing market needs. This may be particularly true of universities with an urban campus for which open admissions and no or low tuition to the city universities and community colleges create formidable competition. Clemens University, for one, is proud of its record of new programs and has, in fact, a repution in the state capitol for aggressive, successful efforts. Chase University is acknowledged to be an example of an entrepreneurial university actively seeking new markets and new students by a variety of programs as unique as an MBA for Brazilian business managers, joint degree programs with other institutions and courses in neighboring corporations during working hours.

Such continual creation of new programs, variations of older programs and withdrawal of unsuccessful programs must create an atmosphere of constant uncertainty in collection maintainance and development in the libraries of the campuses affected. In the haste to expand, adequate library preparation was frequently overlooked in the institutions surveyed; it appears that where adequate funds were not available for extensive collection building, libraries were not drawn into planning for new programs. Programs were announced without consultation with the director of libraries and without supplemental funds to strengthen the collections to support the new programs. Few moves to reach out for new markets by Clemens and Chase involved the libraries in advance planning with the result that in some instances new programs were instituted, students requested materials and the libraries were unprepared. The outgoing chief of the Thoreau library of Clemens University, for example, was particularly bitter about lack of library participation in academic planning on that campus during his tenure. A new directive from the senior vice-president /university provost of Emerson campus of that university promising funds to that library in advance of new programs remains to be tested--particularly after his resignation from that position. At Chase University the university librarian also could recall few instances of additional funds for new programs (only one for a new nursing program several years ago) nor could the chief of the Dupont campus (the original campus) recall any advance notice of new programs.

Harrison University may feel no need for entrepreneurial and expansionary efforts; as a state-related university it has the comfort of knowing that one-third of its income is derived from the state and that the state will be a friend of last resort should calamitous events befall it. Other considerations: because of state financial support, Harrison's tuition can be kept competitive, making it less vulnerable to other competi-

Summary and Conclusions 237

tion, and its commitment to the state to
offer high-level programs to community college graduates means a virtually assured
level of new students. Yet Harrison has not
entirely ignored the need to cultivate new
sources of income. It opened a satellite
campus in the city downtown, aware that the
potential that exists there would not travel
the few miles to the main campus located in
an economically depressed area, and to generate students overseas it recently established
a business school in Japan.

--It would appear that if a university
administration is slow to include its library
director in such program planning processes
as do exist, the library director is obligated to demand it. A library director who
does not sit on the council of deans or its
equivalent may by default lose the opportunity to participate in academic planning or
speak for the library system in such planning. One would hope that university administrations would recognize this and make such
participation mandatory. At Harrison University it was not until 1979 that the director
of libraries was seated on the council of
deans and thereby privy to university academic planning. At Clemens University on
only one campus (Emerson) has the campus library chief been a participant in campus governance. In these universities the administration and leading academic officer have set
the policies for such participation--in each
instance, based upon their conception of the
importance of library involvement in academic
planning.

--When a university does not have the
protective shield of a large endowment and
tuition constitutes the greater part of its
income, the rise and fall of enrollment
quickly forces contraction or expansion of
the library budget. In each of the institutions examined for this study, this has been

shown. Two of the institutions studied (Clemens and Chase) are approximately 85% tuition-dependent with small endowments. As each year's budget is predicated upon that year's projected enrollment, campus and library budget cuts are made immediately if that enrollment does not materialize. As a result, for several years it has not been possible to purchase equipment at Chase University or at the campus libraries of Clemens University. This has been true also in recent years at Harrison University, where some state financial assistance is assured but insufficient to bolster library budgets. Little long-term systemwide planning appears to have been undertaken by any of the libraries in the universities studied; this may be due to uncertain financial conditions that exist each year in institutions that are tuition-driven.

--A new administration or an administrative reorganization often brings with it a new perspective and a re-evaluation of existing goals. At Harrison University, with the appointment of a new director of libraries, the university administration is rectifying previous injustices and inadequacies in the libraries' budgets in a drive to raise the rank of the libraries in the ARL Index; the administration had not acknowledged the need for financial support and involvement with the library before. At Clemens University the new president is determined to bring together a fragmented institution into a unified university--a goal he feels can be advanced by first strengthening the library system. In both instances, a university has recognized the importance of providing financial support for adequate library resources after periods of neglect. It may take near-crisis situations to make university administrations aware of that need.

Summary and Conclusions 239

--The importance of university-wide collection management is rarely acknowledged and acted upon until strong motivation is present. Collection development at Harrison University in the past has been erratic, with little consideration of academic priorities and no long-term planning. Discretionary funds were rarely available after standing orders had been placed and approval plans filled. Enrollment problems in the late 1970s may have been responsible. Also the administration of the university appeared to have little interest in developing collections. This has now changed as a one-time allocation of $1,000,000 has been made for the library to improve its ranking in the ARL Index. However, sudden bounty may not be the most effective way to develop a significant research collection. Advance planning yesterday would assist the library to spend wisely today. To have been through a time when funds for equipment as basic as microfilm reader-printers were not available and now have the opportunity to purchase extensively may be intoxicating, but without time to research carefully its projected needs and available resources, expenditures now may not be the most efficient method to utilize these funds.

--As a matter of convenience, campus libraries in a multicampus library system tend to exchange materials and information with nearby non-system libraries in preference to using other, more distant campus libraries in the system. It would seem that library collection development should take into consideration available library resources nearby--particularly with the long-term prospect of declining enrollment and fiscal restraint. Larger may not always be synonomous with better; it is possible, for example, that it was not advisable for a university with enrollment difficulties (Clemens University) to pour funds into collection building of the

Thoreau campus when the public library's business library, one of the best in the country, is but a few blocks away. Possibly the future of library collection building in smaller and private multicampus institutions may lie increasingly in corsortia agreements and cooperative arrangements with neighboring institutions.

--The sharing of information and resources is expanding rapidly with the acceptance of computer technology. As technology enters the picture more, decisions of centralization or decentralization will become less important. In the meantime, the trend appears to be toward centralized administration and centralized technical services. Harrison University of the universities examined has the only library system where all technical services are performed centrally. At Clemens University, where the eastern division of three libraries has centralized technical services, the director of libraries, at the direction of the new president, plans to introduce centralization to the western region as soon as funds become available for more staff.

At Chase University where each campus library is responsible for its own technical services, the university librarian explained that each campus library chief would be loath to give up that function and no campus library is at present large enough to perform centrally all technical services for all campus libraries. The university librarian's explanation may be the result of a certain reluctance to undertake such a major change since historically it has never been attempted. Possibly with future automation greater centralization can be achieved among the technical services staff of all three campuses of Chase; it would, however, take the unreserved conviction of the importance

Summary and Conclusions

of such a move by the university librarian to accomplish such coordination.

--Perception of strong leadership contributes to leadership itself; perception of a lack of leadership undermines what leadership exists. The lack of leadership may have allowed the difficulties the Thoreau campus of Clemens University has experienced. Personnel conflicts of the staff of that library have been long-standing, with people in neighboring departments who have not spoken to each other in years. (At one point two sets of the National Union Catalog were purchased and placed in adjacent rooms because the acquisitions librarian would not speak to the circulation librarian.) A strong library chief would have soon stopped the continuous strife within the small library staff. It is an appearance of strong leadership that encourages the growth of a strong relationship between a campus chief and a campus administrator. A perception of strong leadership by the university director of libraries can tie the campus libraries together and encourage participation by the campus chiefs in long-range planning. Where such leadership exists today (Chase, Harrison), a cohesive library system is in place. Where such leadership is new (Clemens), a cohesive library system is growing.

--A key component in theories of institutional management, planning--both short range and long range--seems to have been largely irrelevant to the development of the multicampus universities studied here. The planning process, where it exists, has tended to be frustrated by the constant state of change in the institutions. Their lack of a firm financial base, their heavy dependence on tuition, and thus the market-driven nature of their programs have made effective planning difficult, even for more than two years ahead. Improvisation and adaptation to changing circumstances are the hallmarks of these institutions.

The importance of the early seminal work by Lee and Bowen in providing a model for the study of similar institutions must be acknowledged as a basis for this study of multicampus university libraries. Many of the characteristics and differences used by them to distinguish the types and problems in multicampus universities were applicable to these multicampus libraries studied. A longitudinal study should be undertaken to examine the change, if any, that will occur over a longer period of time in the multicampus university libraries investigated. Of interest will be whether the development of the campus libraries will result in greater centralization or in decentralization in library administration and organization--centralized with a strong central administration and with each local campus maintaining a minimum level of local autonomy, or decentralized with a maximum level of local autonomy at each local campus while the central administration functions in a coordinating capacity. As the disclaimer in Lee and Bowen's inquiry states: "None of the alternative patterns of organization is better or worse in abstract. They take shape and can be evaluated only in terms of the environment within which they are set."[2] It must be emphasized that this study is not a judgmental investigation but an examination of the environment within which each multicampus library functions.

This is a fitting place to quote a conclusion by Lee and Bowen:

> We have glimpsed the life of the multicampus ... appreciating that even while we studied each university, it was changing before our eyes .... Nevertheless, common elements can be found in them all. We end the investigation with

Summary and Conclusions

more confidence than when we started in our conviction that the multicampus university is a highly significant way of organizing higher education.[3]

It is this researcher's conviction that in its support of a university's mission, the multicampus library as a system plays a significant contributory role[4]--a culmination of fifty years of experiment and growth.

Notes

[1] Lee and Bowen's definition of a multicampus university specifies "a separate systemwide chief executive with the academic-administrative title of president or chancellor ... interposed between the campus executives and the governing board ..." The Multicampus University, p. 65.

[2] Lee and Bowen, Ibid, pp. 421-422.

[3] Lee and Bowen, Ibid, p. 383.

[4] When the new president assumed his office in the federated system of Clemens University in July 1985, the first appointment he made with the goal of creating a centralized university was that of a university director of libraries, describing this move as starting at the core of the university, the library system. "Memorandum For: The Library Faculty and Staff of [Clemens] University; From: _____, President.

BIBLIOGRAPHY

Beach, Dale S. Personnel: the Management of People at Work. 5th ed. New York: Macmillan, 1985.

Birenbaum, William M. Overlive; Power, Poverty and the University. New York: Dell Publishing Co., 1969.

Bruno, J. Michael. "Decentralization in Academic Libraries." Library Trends 19 (January 1971): 311-317.

Carnegie Commission on Higher Education. Governance of Higher Education; Six Priority Problems. New York: McGraw-Hill, 1973.

Carnegie Commission on the Future of Higher Education. Less Time, More Options: Education Beyond the High School: A Special Report and Recommendations by the Carnegie Commission on Higher Education. New York: McGraw-Hill, 1971.

"Centralization and Decentralization in Academic Libraries: A Symposium." College & Research Libraries 22 (September 1961): 327-340, 398.

"Centralization or Decentralization of Library Collections: A Symposium." Journal of Academic Librarianship 9 (September 1983): 196-202.

Churchwell, Charles D. "The Library in Academia: An Associate Provost's View." In New Dimensions for Academic Library Service, pp. 21-33. Edited by E. J. Josey. Metuchen, N.J.: Scarecrow Press, 1975.

Creswell, John W.; Roskens, Ronald W.; and Henry, Thomas C. "A Typology of Multicampus Systems." *Journal of Higher Education* 56 (January/February 1985): 26-37.

Goodall, Leonard E. "Intercampus Relations in Multicampus Universities." In *Crisis in Campus Management: Case Studies in the Administration of Colleges and Universities*, pp. 53-68. Edited by George J. Mauer. New York: Praeger Publishers, 1976.

Henderson Algo D. and Henderson, Jean Glidden. "Interinstitutional Coordination, Multicampus Systems." In *Higher Education in America*, pp. 218-235. San Francisco: Jossey-Bass Publishers, 1974.

Holley, Edward G. "Organization and Administration of Urban University Libraries." *College & Research Libraries* 33 (May 1972): 175-189.

Keys, Robert C. "An Analysis of Decision-Making Patterns in Public Multicampus Institutions of Higher Education: An Empirical Model." Ph.D. dissertation, Arizona State University, 1976.

Lake, Patrick Roy. "Common Problems in Organizing and Developing Multicampus Community Colleges." Ph.D. dissertation, Indiana University, 1979.

Lee, Eugene C. and Bowen, Frank M. *Managing Multicampus Systems: Effective Administration in an Unsteady State*. San Francisco: Jossey-Bass Publishers, 1975.

Lee, Eugene C. and Bowen, Frank M. *The Multicampus University: A Study of Academic Governance*. New York: McGraw-Hill, 1971.

Levinson, Harry; Molinari, Janice; and Spohn, Andrew G. Organizational Diagnosis. Cambridge, Mass.: Harvard University Press, 1972.

McDonald, John P. "The Rutgers University Library: A Study of Current Problems of Organization and Service in a Decentralized University." In Studies in Library Administrative Problems: Eight Reports from a Seminar in Library Administration, pp. 95-132. New Brunswick, N.J.: Rutgers University, Graduate School of Library Service, 1960.

Miller, James L., Jr. "Coordination Versus Centralized Control." In The Expanded Campus, pp. 237-244. Edited by Dyckman W. Vermilye. San Francisco: Jossey-Bass Publishers, 1972.

Myrick, William J., Jr. Coordination: Concept or Reality? A Study of Libraries in a University System. Metuchen, N.J.: Scarecrow Press, 1975.

Neal, James G. and Smith, Barbara J. "Library Support of Faculty Research at the Branch Campuses of a Multi-Campus University." Journal of Academic Librarianship 9 (November 1983): 276-280.

Parker, Garland G. "Fifty Years of Collegiate Enrollments: 1919-20 to 1969-70." School & Society 98 (Summer 1970): 282-295.

"Report of the Provost's Task Force on University Libraries." Pennsylvania State University, September 18, 1981. (Typewritten.)

"Rutgers University Libraries Master Plan." Prepared by the University Master

Planning Committee on Libraries, May 1, 1979. (Typewritten.)

 Ryan, Donald L. "Libraries in Off-Campus Units." Library Trends 10 (April 1962): 541-551.

 Sammartino, Peter. Multiple Campuses. Rutherford, N.J.: Fairleigh Dickinson University Press, 1964.

 Tauber, Maurice F. "Introduction." In "Centralization and Decentralization in Academic Libraries: A Symposium." College & Research Libraries 22 (September 1961): 327-328.

 U.S. National Center for Educational Statistics. Library Statistics of Colleges and Universities, 1977: Institutional Data. Washington, D.C.: National Center for Educational Statistics, 1980.

 U.S. Office of Education. Library Statistics of Colleges and Universities, 1963-64: Analytic Report. Washington, D.C.: National Center for Educational Statistics, 1968.

 Van Pallandt, Sean. "A Descriptive Study of Systemwide Self-Studies of Multicampus University Systems." Ph.D. dissertation, University of Tennessee, 1981.

 Waymer, William Wade. "A Study of the Actual and Needed Involvement of Central Administrations of Multicampus Systems of Higher Education in the Accrediting Process." Ph.D. dissertation, Florida State University, 1979.

 Woodsworth, Anne. "Decentralization is the Best Principle of Organization Design Where It Fits." In "Centralization or Decentralization of Library Collections: A

Symposium." *Journal of Academic Librarianship* 9 (September 1983): 198-199.

Full documentation will be found in the dissertation on file at Columbia University.

APPENDIX

SAMPLE INTERVIEW QUESTIONNAIRE

Interviews were structured by selecting questions from the following questionnaire guideline appropriate to the area of responsibility of the interviewee.

I. <u>Organization and governance of the parent body</u>

--Physical location of the parent body

--Number and location of the campuses

--Location in relation to each other; accessibility of each campus to other campuses

--Description of the physical plants

--Have significant changes occurred in the organization of the university proper?

--What is the degree of autonomy of each campus? Is the system an example of a consolidated system with influence evenly distributed among the member institutions or is the system a flagship system with one campus favored over the others, such as a main campus and lesser ones?

--Do all member campuses have an equal opportunity to secure resources from the system's central administration?

--How have the campuses dealt with expansion? With contraction?

--What are the sources of financial support, the dependence of the university upon state funding, private endowments?

--Is there an element of political tension among the campuses? And is this reflected within the library system?

II. Organization, governance and administrative structure of the libraries

--What is the reporting relationship of the university librarian, or, if such a position does not exist, the directors of the campus libraries to the university administration?

--What are the degrees of autonomy for each campus library?

--Do the campus libraries constitute a system? Are they interrelated and do they work together as a system?

--Is there a system-wide mission and goals statement for the libraries?

--Has each campus library developed and retained a distinct identity?

--Are specialized curricula concentrated on particular campuses? Are the library resources supportive of such specialization and concentration?

--How do the libraries provide the resources across the entire system for cooperative multicampus degrees and programs?

--Are local policies for purchasing materials and equipment made within the framework of stated system-wide policies or university priorities, as well as the program needs of the individual campuses?

Appendix

--Is the library system included in a system-wide academic plan? Does this plan consider changing student needs, campus emphases, enrollment trends?

--Has a change in the composition of the student body occurred? (e.g., more foreign students, more part-time students). Has this affected the library collections and services? The use of the library?

--Are the libraries included in the preparation of specific new program proposals or reviews of existing programs? At what point in the process of obtaining approval for development of new programs are the libraries involved?

--How are priorities established for the campus libraries within the system?

--What is the relationship between the campus librarians and the campus academic departments?

--If there is a university librarian, what is the relationship of each campus librarian to the campus administrative officer? What are the lines of authority and reporting? Is the primary obligation of the campus library director to the campus administrator or to the university library director?

--What is the balance between centralization and local campus authority?

--What is the organizational structure and internal administration of each campus library?

--What are the lines of authority and reporting within each library?

--What is the relationship between the library administration and the professional staff within each library?

--How are administrative policies and procedures developed and implemented within each library?

--Are library standards and operating procedures uniform within the system?

--What are the processes and agencies of decision-making? What decisions are made at the system-wide level? What kinds of decision-making remain at the campus level?

--What is the role of the professional staff in the planning and program development of each campus library?

--Are personnel policies relating to promotion requirements, staff development, pay scales, benefits, appeals, etc. uniform for all system libraries?

--Can librarians move with relative ease from a position in one library to another within the system?

Library budget process

--What is the ratio of library expenditures to the total institutional expenditures?

--Is there a single budget for all the university's libraries?

--To what extent does the individual library exercise direct control over budget formation and expenditures of its approved budget?

Appendix

--What is the process for planning, developing, and administering the annual budget?

--Has the library budget for acquisitions kept pace with the rising costs for books and journals?

--Does the system have the flexibility to shift appropriated funds among the campus libraries to meet changing student demand?

Collection development

--By whom are proposals initiated for library development of collections on the individual campuses?

--How are resources allocated? Are funds allocated by formula? On the basis of assessment of current needs?

--Is consideration given to programs that have a high priority, the types of programs served, or the differing costs of materials by disciplines?

--Is there a coordinated collection development policy? Is there a written policy?

Cooperation and coordination

--What resource sharing procedures exist?

--What is the extent of intercampus communication among libraries?

--What overall policies are there on different aspects of library services - e.g., technical services, reference services?

--To what degree is there coordination of services and collections with other libraries in geographic or regional networks?

--What are the access policies? Do all members of the university community have access to all of the university's libraries?

Technical services and automation

--What has been the role of new technology and network environment on the libraries on a system-wide basis?

--Is there system-wide planning for automation?

III. Current problems and future planning

--What problems occurred as the single campus library became a multicampus university library?

--How were these problems addressed?

--What problems currently faced are of most concern?

--What fundamental changes would the library system like to implement in the next five to ten years?

--What seem to be the future directions of the libraries, given the contraction in higher education, diminishing enrollment, changing trends in administration, and technological developments?

--What other considerations have surfaced, often unexpectedly, that are unique to a library system which consists of campuses geographically separated yet administered by one parent body?

--To what extent has the history of the institution and of the libraries themselves played a role in the library?

INDEX

Affiliation agreement 165
"An Analysis of Decision-Making Patterns in
    Public Multicampus Institutions of Higher
    Education: An Empirical Model" 26
Anonymity of individuals and institutions 20
Association of Research Libraries 45, 50, 54
Automation 16, 61, 76, 77, 78, 114, 129,
    142, 187, 200, 201, 205, 217, 229, 240
Autonomy 5, 6, 11, 14, 20, 38, 44, 60, 71,
    78, 127, 146, 147, 171, 172, 187, 203,
    222, 226, 231, 234, 242

Birenbaum, William B. 2
Board of trustees 31, 92, 94, 95, 101, 137,
    159, 163, 168, 172, 182
Bowen, Frank M. 1, 3, 6, 7, 8, 11, 13, 16,
    20, 217, 218, 242
Bruno, J. Michael 5

Carnegie Commission on Higher Education 6
Carnegie Commission on the Future of Higher
    Education 23
Center for Research Libraries 73
Central administration 5, 9, 10, 11, 21, 38,
    46, 95, 96, 105, 144, 146, 148, 221, 240,
    242
Central library administration 15, 59, 60,
    231, 232
Centralization 5, 15, 187, 224, 234, 242
"Centralization and Decentralization in
    Academic Libraries: A Symposium" 24
"Centralization or Decentralization of
    Library Collections: A Symposium" 24
Centralized technical services 59, 120, 200,
    203, 240
Churchwell, Charles D. 23

Index

City University of New York 11
Collection development 16, 65, 67, 129, 132, 190, 192, 193, 206, 217, 227, 230, 239
"Common Problems in Organizing and Developing Multicampus Community Colleges" 27
Comprehensive research university 3, 33, 38, 69, 77, 80
Consolidated systems 1, 20, 102, 144, 171, 172, 202, 218, 222, 224
Consortia 140, 198, 240
Contraction 14, 106, 173, 223, 237
Cooperation and resource sharing 16, 73, 75, 131, 139, 146, 147, 192, 198, 205, 217
Cooperative multicampus degrees and programs 131
Coordinate campus 109
Coordinate degree programs 164
Coordinating agency 5
<u>Coordination: Concept or Reality? A Study of Libraries in a University System</u> 11
"Coordination Versus Centralized Control" 25
Cornell University 1
Council of deans 56, 68, 122, 130, 237
Courier services 121, 131, 139, 144, 204
Creswell, John W. 10

Decentralization 5, 15, 240, 242
"Decentralization in Academic Libraries" 24
"Decentralization Is the Best Principle of Organization Design <u>Where It Fits</u>" 25
Decision-making 9, 58, 60, 61, 78, 127, 149, 182, 222
Departmental libraries 60, 67, 128
Description of the campus libraries 46, 113, 178, 217
Description of the campuses 40, 105, 174, 217
"A Descriptive Study of Systemwide Self-Studies of Multicampus University Systems" 26
Distances between campuses 40, 42, 60, 61, 68, 79, 125, 140, 144, 147, 229, 231
Divisional libraries 47, 48, 79

Endowments 39, 104, 172, 224, 237, 238

Enrollment   2, 4, 13, 29, 33, 39, 42, 51, 53,
    66, 92, 94, 102, 105, 108, 111, 116, 132,
    144, 159, 166, 168, 172, 201, 204, 218,
    220, 222, 228, 237
Entrepreneurship   44, 145, 164, 219, 235, 236
Environment   7, 16, 29, 92, 159, 217, 242
Expenditures   71, 72, 136, 138, 197
Exploratory case method   15, 16
Expansion   14, 39, 43, 94, 118, 143, 167,
    173, 174, 194, 203, 220, 223, 237
Faculty council   171, 189, 190
Faculty library committee   130, 188, 228
Faculty senate library committee   59, 72
Faculty status   134, 183, 194, 228
Faculty union   70, 96, 101, 128, 134, 135,
    194, 227
Fairleigh Dickinson University   8
Federal funds   4
Federated system   95, 96, 101, 146, 148, 222,
    234, 243
"Fifty Years of Collegiate Enrollments: 1919-
    20 to 1969-70"   22
First-generation students   79, 145, 224
Flagship   2, 10, 38, 78, 148, 171, 172, 196,
    218, 221, 229, 231

Geographical distances   61, 141, 147, 196,
    205, 217, 220, 221, 226
Goodall, Leonard E.   9
Governance of Higher Education: Six Priority
    Problems   25

Harvard, John   3
Henderson, Algo D. and Henderson, Jean G.   8
Henry, Thomas C.   10
Heterogeneous public systems   11
Higher Education Act   105
Holley, Edward G.   2
Homogeneous public systems   11

Innovative programming   164, 202, 219
Intercampus communication   140, 141
Intercampus loans   12, 51, 52, 53, 68, 75,
    188, 192, 227

Index

"Intercampus Relations In Multicampus
    Universities" 9
"Interinstitutional Coordination, Multicampus
    Systems" 8
Interlibrary loans 12, 52, 60, 73, 75, 131,
    139, 140, 146, 198
International students 36, 168, 224
Interviews 7, 8, 17, 188, 217

Johns Hopkins University 1

Kerr, Clark 22
Keys, Robert C. 9

Lake, Patrick Roy 10
Law school 32, 35, 45, 49, 171, 176, 207
Law school library 49, 50, 76, 178, 181,
    183, 192, 196, 200, 207
Lee, Eugene C. 1, 3, 6, 7, 8, 11, 13, 16,
    20, 217, 218, 242
Less Time, More Options: Education Beyond the
    High School 23
Levinson, Harry 17
"Libraries in Off-Campus Units" 27
Library budget 16, 66, 67, 71, 135, 196,
    217, 227, 228, 237
"The Library in Academia: An Associate
    Provost's View" 23
Library Statistics of Colleges and
    Universities, 1963-64: Analytic Report
    24
Library Statistics of Colleges and
    Universities, 1977: Institutional Data
    21
"Library Support of Faculty Research at the
    Branch Campuses of a Multi-Campus
    University" 27
Local campus authority 59, 127

Managing Multicampus Systems: Effective
    Administration in an Unsteady State 26
Matrix system 100, 126, 169, 189, 225
McDonald, John P. 13
Michigan-Dearborn 9
Middle income students 98, 145, 219

Miller, James L., Jr.   25
Minority students   35, 36, 77, 97, 105, 144, 224, 230
Molinari, Janice   28
The Multicampus University: A Study of Academic Governance   6
Multicampus university system   1, 2, 3, 6, 7, 10, 13, 20
Multiple Campuses   8
Multiversity   2
Myrick, William J. Jr.   11

Neal, James   12

OCLC (Online Computer Library Center)   45, 118, 220, 229
Off-campus sites   11, 31, 202, 220
Online systems   5, 47, 52, 61, 69, 75, 76, 77, 116, 142, 143, 204, 205, 227, 229
Organization and administration of the university   36, 98, 168, 217
"Organization and Administration of Urban University Libraries"   22
Organization, governance and administrative structure of the libraries   54, 78, 122, 181
Organizational Diagnosis   28
Overlive; Power, Poverty and the University   22

Pallandt, Sean Van   10
Parker, Garland G.   22
Part-time students   33, 98, 145, 168
Pennsylvania State University   12
Personnel policies   16, 70, 134, 194, 217
Planning   13, 14, 41, 43, 61, 69, 70, 72, 77, 101, 108, 126, 128, 130, 136, 138, 142, 148, 180, 187, 188, 196, 201, 202, 204, 241
Political tension   14, 61, 103
Previous Studies   6
Processes   7, 16, 20, 217

Index

"Report of the Provost's Task Force on University Libraries" (Pennsylvania State University) 12
Research Libraries Group 45, 49, 73
Research Libraries Information Network 75
Resident faculty 51, 63, 100, 128, 144, 228, 233
Resident students 51, 100, 108, 233
Retrospective conversion 143, 146, 201, 229
Roskens, Ronald W. 10
"Rutgers University Libraries Master Plan" 13
"The Rutgers University Library: A Study of Current Problems of Organization and Service in a Decentralized University" 13
Ryan, Donald L. 11

Sammartino, Peter 8
Self-study 54, 61
Smith, Barbara J. 27
Spohn, Andrew G. 28
State-related institution 29, 39, 46
Student body 35, 36, 79, 97, 100, 108, 110, 144, 167, 217, 220
"A Study of the Actual and Needed Involvement of Central Administrations of Multicampus Systems of Higher Education in the Accrediting Process" 27

Tauber, Maurice F. 25
Technical services 16, 59, 76, 78, 142, 200, 217, 226
Technology 14, 33, 187, 205, 229, 240
Transportation 41, 51, 167, 174, 177, 181, 200, 221, 226, 232
Tuition-dependent 39, 104, 172, 224, 235, 238
Typology 10, 11, 218
"A Typology of Multicampus Systems" 27

University budget 39, 109, 135, 172, 196, 217, 224, 228
University deans 104, 163, 202, 234
University faculties 96, 104, 222

University librarian 15, 19, 47, 51, 52, 56,
    60, 122, 124, 125, 127, 146, 181, 182,
    203, 219, 225, 234, 238
University library policies 61, 67, 142,
    187, 203, 227
University library system 4, 20, 45, 46, 49,
    69, 54, 61, 70, 72, 73, 74, 75, 78, 124,
    127, 129, 142, 143, 149, 207, 224, 225,
    229
University of Illinois at Chicago 9

Waymer, William Wade 10
Woodsworth, Anne 25

AUG 2 3 1990